Two pounds of mestizo dough

A half pound of filet of Spania

cooked and finely chopped

A pious little box of dried raisins

Two spoons of Malinche milk.

Gently fry conquistador helmets

Three Jesuit onions

A little bag of multinational gold

Two cloves of dragon

A presidential carrot

Two spoons of gossip

...toes

Half a cup of crosshair sugar

Two drops of volcano lava

Seven leaves of penis

(Don't think badly of me, it's a soporific).

Put everything to boil on a low flame

for five hundred years

and see what happens.

—Claribel Alegría

LATIN SPIRIT 365 DAYS
The Wisdom, Landscape and Peoples of Latin America

Danielle & Olivier Föllmi

Foreword by Edmond Mulet
Special Representative of the Secretary General and
Chief of the United Nations Mission for the Stabilization of Haiti (MINUSTAH)

Texts taken from Aymara, Aztec, Guarani, Inca, Kouna, Maya, Puebla, Quechua, and Quitché traditions.

And including Humberto Ak'Abal, Claribel Alegría, Homero Aridjis, Miguel Ángel Asturias, Patricio Atkinson, José Balza, Apolonio Bartolo Ronquillo, Mario Benedetti, Jorge Luis Borges, Cristovam Buarque, Dom Hélder Câmara, Luis Cardoza y Aragón, Ismael Cerna, Paulo Coelho, Francisco Coloane, Rubén Darío, Enrique Dussel, Fabricio Estrada, David Escobar Galindo, Gabriel García Márquez, Otto Raúl González, Nicolás Guillén, Orides Fontela, Carlos Fuentes, Eduardo Hughes Galeano, Thilda Herbillon-Moubayed, Benito Juárez, Roberto Juarroz, Hugo Lindo, Antonio Machado, J.M. Machado de Assis, José Martí, Federico Mayor, Rigoberta Menchú, Gabriela Mistral, Augusto Monterroso, Roberto Monzón, Pablo Neruda, Juan Carlos Onetti, José Emilio Pacheco, Nicanor Parra, Violeta Parra, Octavio Paz, Maria Teresa Perdomo, Quino, Serafín Quiteño, Roberto Resendiz Carmonaz, Augusto Roa Bastos, Jaime Sabines, Luis Sepúlveda, Ralph Thamar, Magdelena Thomson, Mario Vargas Llosa, José Mauro de Vasconcelos, Leopoldo Zea.

Thames & Hudson

To Manolo, to Baltazar, to my dear family,
To the peoples, poets, and martyrs
who defended the glory and the beauty of Latin American culture.

—Danielle Föllmi

IN *DANCE, CONSCIOUSNESS OF LIFE,* Thilda Herbillon-Moubayed writes: "What is 'the fantastic'? A means of escape from a hostile reality? The ability to surrender to the world of play and imagination? Emancipation? An escape? A distanced view used to attain light and nourish oneself with poetry? A vagabond or amorous adventure? An expectation of the exceptional? A transcendence of reality? An admission of the supernatural? A reaction against rationalism? The avowal of the impossibility of acting...? The fantastic is all of that."

Having spent my entire childhood in Latin America, I identify it with this boundlessly inspiring quality of the fantastic. Despite its frequently painful history, this land of mixtures and cultural exchanges continually generates new ideas and vital forces. The wide-ranging sources of Latin American wisdom represented in this book encompass the Latin American soul, the very essence of its multiple identities: the indigenous people of Amazonia; communities of Aztec, Mayan, and Incan ancestry, and the great sacred texts, the *Popol Vuh* and *Chilam Balam;* iconic revolutionaries and philosophers of liberation; and the important Latin American literary tradition, with its acclaimed poetry and fiction, and distinguished writers who have been awarded the Nobel Prize in Literature.

Connecting to our origins, to the Sun and the Pachamama, Mother Earth; refining our senses; developing our creativity; enriching our relationship with ourselves and with others; uniting with the forces of nature; filling ourselves with the energies of the universe: every theme that emerges in this book enriches us with a unique way of conceiving and expressing the world, rethinking the other and ourselves—loving life, our life, in the Latin American way.

Danielle Föllmi

FOREWORD

THE VOLUME IN THE READER'S HANDS is one of the links in the chain that originated in the Himalayas, made its way down to India, and passed through Africa. Following the publication of the three previous volumes in the Offerings for Humanity series, replete with their astonishing visual testimony and profound texts, we are given this book. It will precede books in the series on the wisdom of the Far East, Middle East, and the Occident, giving new form and meaning to the chain of civilizations, of humankind.

This book is neither reportage nor a documentary. It is a book of photographic art—of portraits and places—created by a witness who lived with our people and breathed with them the "breath of the time." In Guaraní, the word for "wisdom" is *sarandú*, which means "sensing the time." The spirit and thought, the imaginative power and creativity of the people of Latin America, amassed in the works of their great Latin American poets, writers, and thinkers, are evoked by these photographs in a magical communion never before achieved in this continental scope and breadth.

These images highlight life as experience, not affliction. Even in places where poverty and despair reign, the authors find dignity—dignity in the glance. In some photographs the author gives expression to commonplace scenes without romanticizing them—to the dignity of labor, of daily tasks.

In these pages we also find our *joie de vivre*, sunny smiles, music, and dance. The variety of music and expression in movement found in Latin America is unmatched, and we marvel at the hip-swinging images, reflecting an important aspect of our being.

In these pages we also find our *joie de vivre*, sunny smiles, music, and dance. The variety of music and expression in movement found in Latin America is unmatched, and we marvel at the hip-swinging images, reflecting an important aspect of our being.

Latin America, which is becoming conscious of its identity and of its natural beauty and wealth, is on its way to self-respect and to their preservation. Works such as this one contribute in marking out our path. The images in this book belong to today, not to the past, and show us, without nostalgia, what our future can be: luminous, full of color—particularly green—the one generous Mother Earth that exists for everyone. The *Popol Vuh* tells us that "in nature nothing and nobody is superfluous." The sun, the earth, the water—all of nature's elements, which we venerate—are celebrated in full measure.

Color is represented in such profusion because we are so fond of it—the multicolored textiles of the mountain people, the carnival makeup, the picturesque facades of the houses and churches, the variegated cloud banks at sunset. Immersed in this rainbow of colors are the bronze, white, and black mestizo peoples, particularly the descendants of the great Olmec, Aztec, Maya, and Inca civilizations, with their copper-colored skin, smooth in children and, in old people, revealing furrows that extend to the soul.

There are those among us who question the existence of a Latin American essence or character, whereas others encounter and esteem it. In reflecting on his experiences in so many communities in our hemisphere—there, "where he breathed the time," Olivier Föllmi told me: "More than anywhere else, it's all here." His photographs, together with the powerful thoughts and words of our writers, imaginatively selected by Danielle Föllmi, constitute a pure and generous offering for Latin America and a momentous revelation for the world.

Edmond Mulet

Special Representative of the Secretary General
and Chief of the United Nations Mission
for the Stabilization of Haiti (MINUSTAH)

In our language, wisdom is called "arandù," which means "to feel time."

—Guarani people of Amazonia

Luisana, sixteen years old, a member of the Sarayaku community in the Amazon rain forest of Ecuador.

The sun rises—ancestral lion, paternal and central force of our universe.

Night plates the oceans with silvery scales. Meteors trail celestial phosphorus. Sun, water, spring

give us our daily bread. A prayer is born. A poem is born.

—Pablo Neruda

Sunset on the Caribbean coast of Jamaica.

"Come, small life, spark of light,

take the wings of the earth,"

you are the son of honey and of the sixth sun,

you will carry your light to the world…

and to light you will return.

—Amerindian oral tradition, inspired by Pablo Neruda

A group of young Indians perpetuate their Aztec cultural heritage on the Zócalo, Mexico City's central plaza.

It was you, sovereign of all twilights,

who designed the feathers of birds,

the swirl of their flight, the trill of their song.

It was you, mistress and giver of life,

of the gift of breath and movement,

who would assign the sun its course,

the night its shadows, and the tribes their dance.

—Otto Raúl González

Celebrating carnival in Salvador da Bahia, Brazil.

Every day you play with the light of the universe.

—Pablo Neruda

The macaw of Guatemala.

We walk along under the absolute monarchy of the sun.

There is complete harmony between being here and being alive.

—José Emilio Pacheco

Agripina, an Aymara Indian, goes to gather her sheep near Peru's Lake Titicaca, 12,500 feet (3,800 m) above sea level.
Following pages: Salar de Uyuni in Bolivia, the largest salt flat in the world.

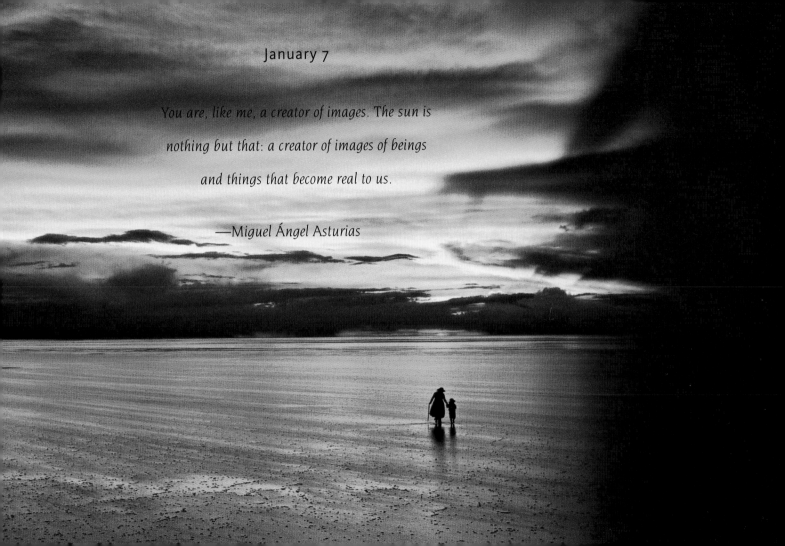

January 7

You are, like me, a creator of images. The sun is

nothing but that: a creator of images of beings

and things that become real to us.

—Miguel Ángel Asturias

As water the sky comes down to the earth....

Germinal planetary passion dissolves in the din of drums.

The sky opens and the sun beams upon the limpid electric air....

The trees are roused from their lethargy.

—Luis Cardoza y Aragón

Tikal—meaning "place of echoes" in Maya Quitché—is the largest religious metropolis of the Mayan world;
it rises out of the heart of the Petén rain forest in Guatemala.

It is not the last wave with its salty weight

that pulverizes coasts and produces

the sandy peace that envelops the world:

it's the central volume of force,

the extended potency of waters,

the motionless solitude brimming with life.

—Pablo Neruda

The fjords leading to the San Rafael lagoon in Patagonia, Chile.

It is raining so hard, so fervently, on the amorously reclining earth!

The approaching sun shower rattles the space from the chicle tree to the

fine shade grasses like a blind harp stirs the forest, whipping between the stones,

green with moss and mushrooms, lichens and lianas.

—Luis Cardoza y Aragón

Tropical rain forest beneath the highly active 8,500-foot-high (2,552-m) Pacaya volcano in Guatemala.

See rose, bee purer than dreams,

almond-eyed woman transformed from the roots of an oak filled with songs

into form, strength of foliage with nests,

mouth of tempests, exquisite sweetness

that would seduce the light with her hips.

—Pablo Neruda

In Brazil, a young vendor in Salvador da Bahia's old city.

Surfstar,

mother water,

mother matter,

invincible medulla.

—Pablo Neruda

The tail of a cyclone over the Caribbean.

Lovers close their eyes at the peak of the kiss.

The night opens for them and restores what has been lost.

—Octavio Paz

Virgin tropical rain forest in Fuentes Georginas, Guatemala.
Following pages: A young woman bathes in the Rio Bobonaza in Sarayaku.

January 14

To exist is to spread out, to overflow, to turn liquid, to return to

the primordial water, to the ocean that is the mother of all.

—Octavio Paz

Mother Earth

I *study you with the anxiety of one who saw you who knows when.*

I *study you like one blindly in love since birth.*

—Luis Cardoza y Aragón

A peasant woman heads home in the mountains of Sucre, Bolivia.

We acquire lizard eyes and set out in the cosmic silence to retrace the millennia.

The vegetative enters into us.

—Luis Cardoza y Aragón

Sea lions in the Galápagos Islands, Ecuador.

My country:

It is a bird song, the language of water,

a cascading syllable, a tempest of crystal ware—

It is the voice of fruits in fragrant springtime,

a fluvial kiss of the forests and the blue mask of the Atlantic.

It is bread on America's table, and the purity of bread on the table.

—Pablo Neruda

In Cartagena, Colombia, single mother Doña Anjelica sells fruit to feed her seven children.

The wind stops and hears the clamor of the elements,

sand and water talking in low voices,

the howl of pilings as they battle the salt,

the rash confidence of fire,

the soliloquy of ashes, the interminable conversation of the universe.

—Octavio Paz

Dawn over Lake Atitlán and the 10,361-foot-high (3,158 m) Tolimán volcano in Guatemala.

Mother of man, herb of tenderness, drowsing water.

Mother of peoples, drowsing herb, water of tenderness,

nothing could be attempted without your help, nothing, nothing:

from your hand welled the dark river of life,

the four main directions of the wind,

the silent lava of the primitive fire,

and the voyage of the waters around the world.

—Otto Raúl González

A peasant woman in the Cordillera Apolobamba of Bolivia returns to her llamas.

The emotion stems not only from the landscape's opulence, but from the spiritual state

it engenders: we move into the three empires and return to the paradisiacal

until we arrive at the first day. The world, charged with a nuptial oblivion, smiles upon us.

A sensation at once of tranquillity and stupor, like that of the coiling reeds and lianas.

—Luis Cardoza y Aragón

Twilight at Bolivia's Salar de Uyuni, the largest salt flat in the world.
Following pages: The tropical rain forest between the Pacific and the high plateaus of Guatemala.

January 21

The underground murmur mingled

with the planetary music of infinite space, the accordions

of the forest, and the chewing of the ants.

—Luis Cardoza y Aragón

Beneath the prairie night the song

of all that I was before I came to be,

of all that we were, has long since rested

on a buffalo skin, in a solemn silence of syllables.

—Pablo Neruda

Cattle returning to their barns in the mountains of Sucre, Bolivia.

I am stronger

because I bear in me

not my little life,

but all the lives,

and I walk steadily forward

because I have a thousand eyes.

—Pablo Neruda

Silvio David Malaver Santi, head of the Sarayaku community in Ecuador, fights to defend the Amazon rain forest.

To all, to you

silent beings of the night

who took my hand in the darkness, to you,

lamps

of immortal light, star lines,

staff of life, secret brethren,

to all, to you,

I say: there's no giving thanks,

nothing can fill the wineglasses

of purity,

nothing can

contain all the sun in the invincible

springtime's flags

like your quiet dignity.

—Pablo Neruda

On the Day of the Dead in Mexico, flowers are placed on graves to honor the deceased.

This is not the first time,

offshoot of humankind bearing firewood

whom you see raising up hope

from the ground. Your hope.

Hope, for you, can arise only from the earth.

—Miguel Ángel Asturias

A porter in the market of San Francisco el Alto, Guatemala.

The blood of everyone finds its course in me, clearing my path through the granite night.

—Luis Cardoza y Aragón

The convent of San Nicolàs Tolentino, founded in 1548, in Actopan, Mexico.

Powers of the light,

now, awake,

with the light in your eyes.

Now, say everything,

with the light on your lips.

Now, go out to the world

with the light of all the yesterdays.

—Fabricio Estrada

Young girl of the Raqchi community on the Altiplano of Peru.
Following pages: Potato fields on Anapia Island on Lake Titicaca, Peru.

Without love for the earth there is no place

for us in heaven.

—*Aymara oral tradition*

Where I am from, but these seedlings,

blue matter that entangles or curls or uproots

or clamorously sows or somnolently spreads,

or climbs and forms the tree's bulwark,

or sinks and binds the copper's cell,

or springs to the river's branch,

or succumbs in the coal's buried stock,

or gleams in the grape's green darkness.

—Pablo Neruda

The peacock, a sacred animal for Indian communities in Bolivia.

Damp green is this coat of stone,

this breeze of numbers and lunar months,

damp green is this coat of stone,

eternity in quetzal feathers,

damp green is this coat of stone.

—Miguel Ángel Asturias

Scratched into the desert of Peru, the geometric figures of Nazca—the earliest dating back to 300 BC—remain veiled in mystery.

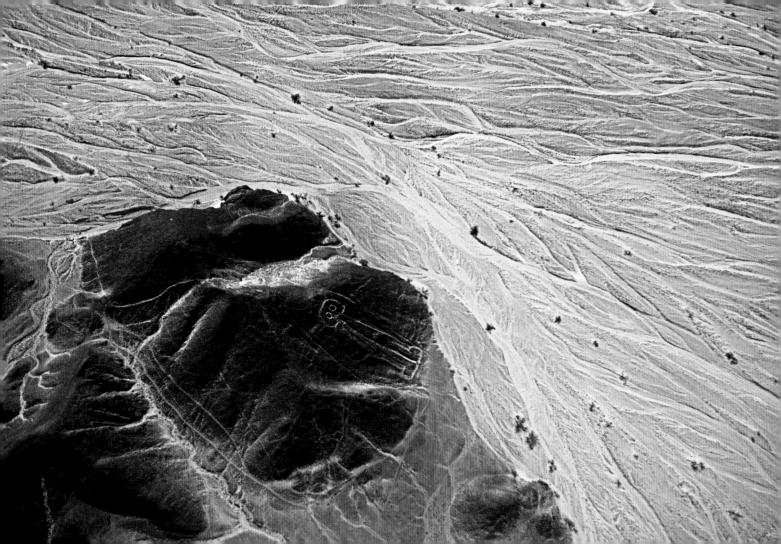

Physical beauty resides in the most profound reaches of matter, in the structure

and harmony of the skeleton, image of death. For me, its features arise from the living

and hidden mineral structure, harking back as far as the obsidian skin to the sun.

—Luis Cardoza y Aragón

The Barrara dance troupe rehearses in an abandoned courtyard in Havana, Cuba.

Thanks be to life that gave me so much.

It gave me two eyes, and when I open them,

I can perfectly distinguish black from white,

And up there in the sky, a layer of stars,

And from among the multitudes, the man I love.

Thanks be to life that gave me so much.

—Violeta Parra

At the vegetable market in Zunil, Guatemala.

The first stirrings of man must have been dance and the language of poetry.

With these instruments, man expresses his fears and his hopes,

he makes his invocations and tries to communicate.

—Jorge Luis Borges

Sculpture at the National Museum of Anthropology in Mexico City, where the treasures of the Olmecs, Toltecs, Mayas, Mexica, and Aztecs are displayed.

A *passing* sound.

The fleeting sound of a profound miracle.

I am, of course, more than the mysterious flesh

in which someone once brought me into the world.

—David Escobar Galindo

A festive crowd at carnival in Salvador da Bahia, Brazil.

Following pages: Dusk over Fisherman's Island in Salar de Uyuni, Bolivia, the largest salt flat in the world at 4,085 square miles (10,582 km²).

Life, truth, light, triple flame

born of the intimate, infinite flame.

—Rubén Dario

Myth hatches feathered monsters everywhere loaded with death and wisdom,

with all the prenatal pain. It is a logbook, a compass.

—Luis Cardoza y Aragón

Among the many groups promoting their cultures on the Zócalo in Mexico City, a group of young Indians imparts Aztec tradition.

It was other roots and seeds in the soil,

this act of laying seedbeds in the humus,

out of horror of hunger, time, and death;

this act of dividing the waters into arteries,

out of horror of drought, time, and death;

this act of pampering the moon with one's eyes,

out of horror of darkness, time, and death.

—Miguel Ángel Asturias

In the courtyard of an old colonial home in Antigua, Guatemala.

It's not that stones are dumb; they just keep quiet.

—Humberto Ak'Abal

Detail of a colossal Olmec head on display at the National Museum of Anthropology in Mexico City.

Zapata will live as long as people believe that they have

a right to their land and a right to govern themselves

according to their deeply held beliefs and cultural values.

—Carlos Fuentes

A tobacco farmer in the Viñales Valley, Cuba.

Poetry is rebellion.

My faith in all the future's harvests is affirmed in the present.

And I declare that poetry is indestructible. It may shatter into

a thousand fragments, but it will become crystal again. Poetry was born

with man and will continue to sing for man. It will sing. We will sing.

—Pablo Neruda

The garden of an early convent in the old colonial quarter of Cartagena, Colombia.

This clarity will bring forth farms, cities, mines

and this unity, like the cultivated and blossoming earth,

will give rise to a creative permanence,

the germ of a new city for our times.

—Pablo Neruda

The village of Maragua in the mountains of Sucre, Bolivia.
Following pages: Ears of corn drying under the canopy of a house in Xecul, Guatemala.

February 11

We walk.

We enter

the natural temple of corn,

feet shod with mud.

There is no greater reverence!

—Humberto Ak'Abal

Here is a pulsation,

beginning of another expression of life:

an initial movement

in the silken intimacy of a cocoon,

a babbling that is not yet a word,

a tuning of rare instruments

that seeks to open the flow

of a melody

in the slow awakening

of a stem in the seed,

a radiance, debut of a dawn

about to be born.

—María Teresa Perdomo

Napping in the shade of a hut in Sarayaku in Ecuador's Amazon rain forest.

She:

The farthest stars are entangled in your arms. I am afraid.

Forgive my not having arrived sooner.

He:

A smile from you erases all of the past.

Your sweet lips shelter what is already far away.

—Pablo Neruda

Jennifer and Luis declare their love in the old convent of Santa Catalina in Arequipa, Peru.

Closed space needs to be justified, rationalized;

open space appeals to the senses.

The one imprisons the person in a system,

the other engenders a spiritual outlook,

a "horizon of the soul."

—Gladys Olivera Grotti

Potato farming in the Urubamba Valley of Peru.

O floating freedom

O sea of sounds, of forms, of radiance,

Viva, fountain of being!

Suspended delight without memory,

I forget that you revive the forgotten.

I choke in your riches

and find myself in your waves.

All that I contemplate, contemplates me.

And I am at once fruit and lips,

whatever is constant and is fleeting.

—Octavio Paz

In the old colonial quarter of Cartagena, Colombia.

Only the word—clay. Not spoken. Made. Shaped. Clay of dreams.

Dark clay, spoken with the fingers. I create and I believe. I create because I believe,

and I believe because I create. Whoever believes, creates. Whoever creates, believes.

Fingers in the clay. I believe. I create because I believe in the clay, I create with the clay.

—Miguel Ángel Asturias

One of many churches in the old colonial quarter of Sucre, Bolivia.

Your body is the place of every memory,

A privileged place, the junction of Matter,

Energy, Spirit, and Conscience,

The entire universe is in your body,

your body is a Temple.

—Amazonian oral tradition

Reiner Cutipa Amau, one month and sixteen days old, in Paucartambo province, Peru.
Following pages: Relics of the Maya ceremonial center in Palenque, Mexico.

February 18

Time is no longer succession and becomes what it originally was and is:

the present, in which past and future are reconciled.

—Octavio Paz

The cardinal points are five:

you, here, are

the fifth cardinal point.

—Humberto Ak'Abal

A young girl in Havana, Cuba, celebrates the anniversary of the birth of poet José Martí.

The simple things are the most extraordinary ones,

and only the wise are able to see them.

—Paulo Coelho

A father takes his son to school in old Antigua, Guatemala.

Thanks be to life that gave me so much.

Life let me walk with tired feet;

And so I crossed cities and swamps,

Beaches and deserts, mountains and plains,

To your house, your street, your courtyard.

Thanks be to life that gave me so much.

—Violeta Parra

Sitting at 12,500 feet (3,812 m) above sea level, Lake Titicaca's Anapia Island is home to 280 families.

God is where you let him in.

—Latin American oral tradition

Observing Holy Week in Antigua, Guatemala.

To love is to have eyes in one's fingertips,

to touch the knot tied

by stillness and motion.

—Octavio Paz

Alberto Rafael Gonzáles Figueroa, a dance teacher in Antigua, Guatemala, with student Claudia Lucia Diaz López.

Outside the world is eternal.

Inside time is regurgitated,

happy hour, seconds of sand

and sleep,

minutes of blinking,

decades of flesh and bone.

—Roberto Monzón

A young Indian girl in Sarayaku, Ecuador, sits out a torrential downpour in her hammock.
Following pages: In the mountains of Tarabuco, Bolivia.

February 25

The true revolutionary is guided by a great feeling of love.

—Che Guevara

That's how you came into the world.

You come from so many places,

from the water and the earth,

from the fire and the snow,

from so far away you journey

toward the two of us,

from the terrible love

that has enchained us,

that we want to know

what you're like, what you say to us,

because you know more

about the world we gave you.

—Pablo Neruda

Shana Gualinga Santi, four months old, in the Amazon rain forest of Ecuador.

Nahual,

hidden god,

secret name,

magical substance,

heaven's seal on our flesh, star,

ultimate reality of our breath.

—Hugo Lindo

On the Caribbean coast of Quintana Roo, Mexico.

Color multiplies, and the eyes are bewildered by the solar orgy pouring on the hive.

We are between mountains and volcanoes damp with dew, sipping honey

and transporting pollen, performing by instinct our primordial cosmic task.

—Luis Cardoza y Aragón

At the wholesale vegetable market, farmers from the Almolonga region of Guatemala stream in to sell vegetables in bulk.

You are the frenzied youth of the bee,

the drunkenness of the wave, the power of the wheat-ear.

—Pablo Neruda

A girl in her grandfather's shop in Chile.

Veneration? There is a subtle relation between veneration and participation:

veneration is already participation. We venerate the world around us,

and at another level, that veneration spreads to all things and living beings,

to stones and trees and animals and humans.

—Octavio Paz

Mayan ruins at the important Tulum archaeological site located on the Caribbean coast of Quintana Roo, Mexico.

Will the sun come out tomorrow?

Will the orb drown in its light,

suffocating in its perpetual fury?

How do you say "Good day" to life?

Don't ask any longer,

There is nothing to say, nothing either to silence.

Thought sparkles, goes forth, returns:

devouring and engendering, it repeats itself;

neither alive nor dead,

always about the cold eye that thinks it.

—Octavio Paz

Cuzco Cathedral, Peru.
Following pages: At the market in Pisac, Peru, in the Sacred Valley.

March 4

At the beginning, mother and light are a single entity.

The child's life, the man's life, is but

a continuation of that light.

—Pablo Neruda

I was born to be born, to remember the steps of all who approach,

of what pounds at my chest like a trembling new heart.

—Pablo Neruda

In the Cuzco region of Peru, an infant naps while his mother sells shawls in the market.

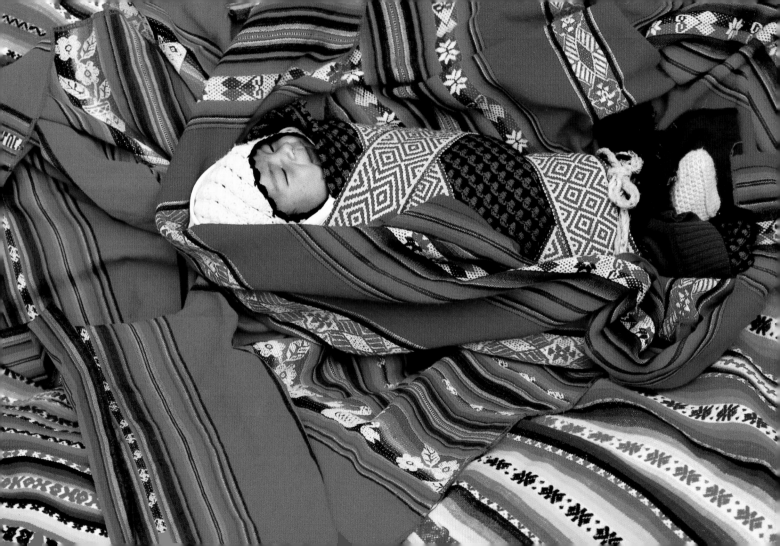

Each of us is human and represents the hopes and possibilities of the species.

—Octavio Paz

A young hunter in Sarayaku practices using his blowpipe.

No matter what he does, every person on earth plays a central role in

the history of the world. And normally he doesn't know it.

—Paulo Coelho

A young popcorn vendor in Potosí, Bolivia.

Living is little

but weighs heavy

like all of being

like all of light

like the concentration of time.

—Orides Fontela

North Seymour Island in the Galápagos, Ecuador.

All of us, absolutely all, have something to say to each other

that is worthy of praise or forgiveness by the other.

—Eduardo Galeano

In an orchestra on the streets of Havana, Cuba.

We who carry our cause in our hearts

are the only ones ready to run every risk.

—Rigoberta Menchú

On the San Rafael glacier during the ascent of Mount Saint Valentine, 13,300 feet (4,058 m) above sea level in Patagonia.
Following pages: Salt harvest on Bolivia's Salar de Uyuni.

One destiny is no better than the next and every man must accept the destiny he bears inside himself.

—Jorge Luis Borges

Father Sun

I want to thank you.

Because you give us light,

because you give us warmth,

no matter to whom.

Father who makes the days possible,

you interrupt the darkness,

light up the way,

open life to us.

Do not neglect us,

protect our steps,

encourage our hope.

—Apolonio Bartolo Ronquillo

A stone sculpture of the rain god called Tlaloc by the Aztecs and Chac Mool by the Maya
on display at the National Museum of Anthropology in Mexico City.

Light winks at me. I respond by winking at it with my shadow.

—Roberto Juarroz

Fishermen setting out at dawn from Lake Titicaca's Anapia Island in Peru.

When your heart beats to bursting,

when your eyes cry every tear,

when your soul sings the essence of your soul,

you are reconciled with the world,

you gently take root.

—Amazonian oral tradition

A child being scolded by his mother in Chivay, in the Colca Valley of Peru.

Our heritage cannot be renounced, but it is yesterday's if we do not transfigure it.

The population is composed of strata foreign to each other, separate and inimical.

Likewise, our life: we are a mosaic of voices, silences, flames, and shadows in a hazy design.

—Luis Cardoza y Aragón

The Andes ascend from the Pacific coast of Peru.

All is presence, all centuries are this present.

Fortunate the eye that does not see because now all is presence,

and its proper vision is to look outside itself.

—Octavio Paz

Interior dome of the Basilica of the Virgin of Guadalupe in Morelia, Mexico.

Thrust in your hand, seize the radiance,

the solar fish, the flame in the blue,

the song that swings in the fiery day.

—Octavio Paz

At sunset in the Salar de Coipasa, Bolivia, a woman tries to flag down a distant vehicle for a ride back to her village.
Following pages: A folkloric troupe dances in front of the village church in Yanque in Peru's Colca Valley.

March 18

I am here to sing this history.

—Carlos Fuentes

We return through the body to the beginning,

spiral off stillness and motion.

Taste, moral knowledge, finite pause,

has beginning and end—and is measureless.

—Octavio Paz

The llama, the typical domestic animal of the high plateaus of the Bolivian Andes.

It is—the body—my earliest design

my first dance

to the tumultuous rhythm of movement,

my temporal delirium of peaceful moments.

—Roberto Monzón

In the old colonial quarter of Cartagena, Colombia.

The body exists and gives weight and shape to our existence.

It causes pain and gives us pleasure; it is not a suit of clothes we are

in the habit of wearing, not something apart from us.

—Octavio Paz

A young surfer on the beach in Bahia, Brazil.

This body where I dwell

and that bears me to my death

with each step taken,

this body, commonplace

but fresh, that in every moment

makes me trust in luck,

otherwise how could I say

stone, paper, scissors,

and how could I enjoy time

past and the sweet present,

and the pain of my dying

like all of us trying to

live without losing our dreams.

—Roberto Monzón

A fresco in Salvador da Bahia, Brazil.

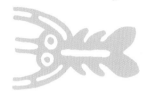

The body, a bridge,

unsteady and unique,

indispensable

for my worldly journey, and the valley

sheltering the reflection

that sparks my conscience.

—Roberto Monzón

Children in Concepción, Bolivia, play in front of a Jesuit mission founded in 1704.

Culture is above all our bodies, our bodies so often sacrificed and denied,

our shackled, dreaming, carnal bodies.

—Carlos Fuentes

A peasant woman on her way back from the market in San Francisco el Alto, Guatemala.
Following pages: Capoeira, an energetic Afro-Brazilian martial art combining dance and wrestling.

March 25

The Church says: The body is a sin.

Science says: The body is a machine.

Advertising says: The body is a business.

The body says: I am a fiesta.

——Eduardo Galeano

Not a song through speech,

but speech through magic.

Promising are its marvels.

—Miguel Ángel Asturias

Claudia, a young Guatemalan mother, with her three-year-old daughter.

The gaucho starts singing in his mother's womb; he is born singing

and he dies singing. And what he sings about, of course,

are his troubles. Only a song can console him in his pain.

—Carlos Fuentes

A street musician in the market of Tarabuco, Bolivia.

The body first appears to our eye as a perfect totality, and yet

it proves to be intangible: the body is always somewhere

beyond the body. On touching it, it divides itself (like a text)

into portions that are momentary sensations.

—Octavio Paz

Twenty-three-year-old Cécilia Antequera Camacho, who was preparing for her wedding in Bolivia.

A *grain of light in a hollow of silence*.

—*Quechua oral tradition*

Colorful cemetery in Chichicastenango, Guatemala.

I *sing to you,*

because you set out on a flight to spheres so distant,

upon a road of stone, of mirrors, of dawns,

with fruit seeds in your hands

and a secret flower of astral lights.

—Roberto Reséndiz Carmona

On a stormy night on the Bolivian Altiplano, a grandmother and her granddaughter return to their village.

There is only one beautiful child in the world and each mother has that one.

—Latin American oral tradition

A Guatemalan child rests with her mother after a dance lesson.
Following pages: The fertile region of Maragua in the mountains of Sucre, Bolivia.

April 1

Nobody or nothing in nature is superfluous.

—Popol Vuh, *Mayan sacred text*

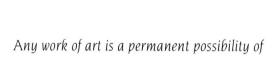

Any work of art is a permanent possibility of

metamorphosis offered to all of mankind.

—Octavio Paz

Hasty service in a restaurant in Kingston, Jamaica.

Because without the outside world

There would be nothing in my consciousness,

but without my inner mirror,

the world would not exist;

for I live through my body, mediating

the walls, mirrors, lakes, sleepless nights

of the world's consciousness.

—Roberto Monzón

Rebeca Gualinga, seventy-three years old, performs a purification rite
on a member of her community in Amazonian Ecuador who is about to take a trip.

April 4

I *am this street's only spectator;*

if I stopped seeing it, it would die.

—Jorge Luis Borges

In the old city of Cuzco, Peru.

How I would love to touch the world with my voice.

Submerge myself in its deep seas

or in the eyes, the even deeper seas,

of an earth woman.

—Otto Raúl González

This detail of a monumental stone sculpture at the National Museum of Anthropology in Mexico City reveals the expressive power of Pre-Columbian art.

For an artist, a tip of a fingernail has a planetary connotation. Rooted in symbols,

human beings take over the world to know it better, to know who they are and where they are.

And to explain the world, investigate it, and invent paths and possibilities.

—Luis Cardoza y Aragón

Violinist Luis Rocha and his grandson Luis, a ten-year-old student organist, in the church of Santa Ana, Bolivia.

Life begins at forty.

So what's the point of having us show up so far ahead of time?

—Quino

April 8

We are condemned to live alone, but also to transcend our solitude,

to re-establish the bonds that united us with life in a paradisiac past.

—Octavio Paz

I *admire two things:*

the harsh law above me

and the starry sky inside me.

—*Orides Fontela*

Cintia Malaver Santi, an eleven-year-old girl from Sarayaku in Amazonian Ecuador.

Pick a big enemy, that will make you grow—so you can take him on.

—Puebla oral tradition, Mexico

A silhouette at the village market in Tarabuco, Bolivia.

But I'm the metallic nimbus, the ring

chained to space, clouds, spheres,

that touches hurtling mute waters,

and again defies the infinite inclemency.

—Pablo Neruda

Chile's still-active Villarrica volcano, 9,338 feet (2,847 m) above sea level.

I *bear in my fiery spirit*

the beautiful light of passionate zeal.

I *love liberty more than life*

and I was not born to bow my head.

—Ismaël Cerna

A young alligator is captured in Sarayaku for release outside the village.

Only because

I err

do I find

what I am not

not looking for.

—Orides Fontela

In Brazil, playing near a fountain in Salvador da Bahia's old city.

We are taught from childhood to accept defeat with dignity,

a conception that is certainly not ignoble.

—Octavio Paz

A resident of Morelia, Mexico.
Following pages: Ascending Mount Saint Valentine, 13,300 feet (4,058 m) above sea level in Patagonia, Chile.

April 15

Fate is a man lured by a destiny, rather than driven by a cause.

—Ernesto Sabato

When you really want something, the universe conspires in your favor.

—Paulo Coelho

A child crosses a bridge to catch the landing of the small single-engine plane that occasionally provides the people of Sarayaku with a connection to the outside world.

We must teach our children to dream

Because with dreams they will know what to believe in.

And when they know what to believe in

They will know why to follow the law—

civic, social, and spiritual.

—Patricio Atkinson

At a children's carnival in Salvador da Bahia, Brazil.

Knowing is no different from dreaming, nor dreaming from doing.

Poetry has set fire to every poem.

Words have been wiped out, images wiped out.

The separation between name and thing is abolished:

to name is to create, and to imagine is to be born.

—Octavio Paz

Detail of textile used by farmers to carry vegetables to market in Zunil, Guatemala.

We must dispel a deep misunderstanding: to know something is not to possess it.

And another: to know is not to understand.

And yet another: knowing is not the opposite of not knowing, but of knowing badly.

Knowing is an approach to being, and should resemble being.

—Roberto Juarroz

Twenty-one-year-old José Luis Gualinga Vargas, an Amazonian Indian, takes an agribusiness exam at his school in Sarayaku, Ecuador.

My language is a language of reflections. A language where I copy

the visible in my white stone mirror. And the invisible in my

black stone mirror. In order to say tree, I collect my mirror saliva

in front of the tree and copy it. To copy is to say. To say is to reflect.

A bird in my mirror is a bird; in copying it I am saying bird.

—Miguel Ángel Asturias

An unusual public telephone on the main plaza of San Miguel de Velasco, Bolivia.

Between being and non-being the grass wavers,

the elements become lighter,

outlines shade over,

glimmers, reflections, reverberations,

flashes of forms and presences,

image mist, eclipse:

what I see, we are: mirages.

—Octavio Paz

At the bus terminal in San Francisco el Alto, Guatemala.
Following pages: At the market in Solola, Guatemala.

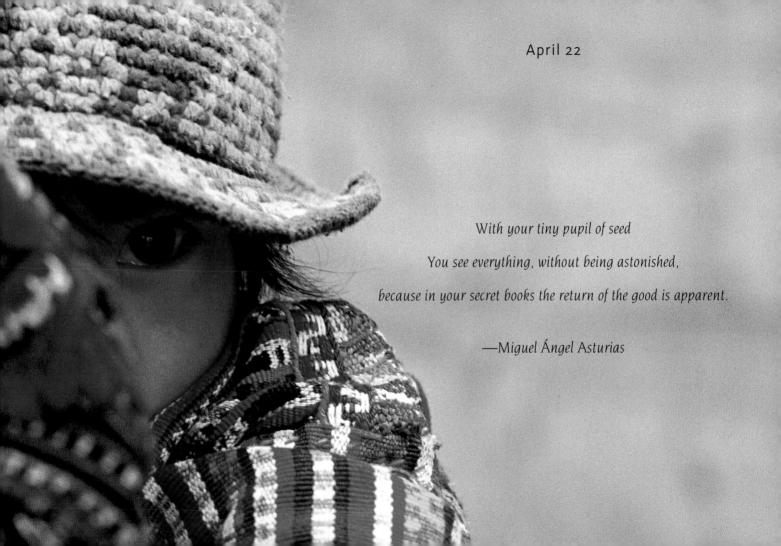

April 22

With your tiny pupil of seed

You see everything, without being astonished,

because in your secret books the return of the good is apparent.

—Miguel Ángel Asturias

To love:

to create a body from a soul,

to create a soul from a body,

to create a you from a presence.

—Octavio Paz

A member of the Barrara dance troupe in Havana, Cuba.

Certain words are like a festival bursting from the surprise of birds.

—Roberto Juarroz

Five-year-old Natalie at the market in Otavalo, Ecuador.

With *freedom*, we also fall into a *boundless abyss*—that of our own selves.

—Octavio Paz

Fishing on the Rio Bobonaza in the Amazon rain forest of Ecuador.

Soon after being born we feel we are a fragment detached

from something more vast and intimate, and a desire to

return to that totality from which we were ripped.

—Octavio Paz

A mother in Amazonian Ecuador brings her young son for a visit to the healer.

Beauty, like happiness, occurs frequently.

Not a day goes by in which we don't, for an instant, live in paradise.

—Jorge Luis Borges

Fisherman's Island in Bolivia's Salar de Uyuni at dusk.

Poetry

scatters eyes on a page,

scatters words on our eyes.

Eyes speak,

words look,

looks think.

—Octavio Paz

A young Brazilian prepares for carnival in Salvador da Bahia.
Following pages: Automobile tracks crossing Bolivia's Salar de Uyuni, the largest salt flat in the world.

April 29

It is one thing to think you are on the right path, and another to think this path is the only one.

Anyway, they are all paths.

—Puebla oral tradition

Tree, you who let the traveler know

the sweetness of your presence

by your cool, ample shade

and the halo of your fragrance:

let my presence be revealed in the fields of life,

the mild, warm influence of a creature blest.

—Gabriela Mistral

Tree near the Jesuit mission of Santa Ana, Bolivia.

Only because

I err

I invent

the labyrinth

the quest

the thing

the reason

for the search

—Orides Fontela

At the market in the village of Tarabuco, Bolivia.

I thrust in my hand to grasp the glowing seed

and plant it in my being:

someday it should grow.

—Octavio Paz

A hot spring on the Tatio plateau in Chile.

Thanks be to life that gave me so much.

It gave me a heart that begins to flow over

When I see the depths of your clear eyes.

Thanks be to life that gave me so much.

—Violeta Parra

A villager in the market of Chivay in the Colca Valley of Peru.

Humankind, my children, is like a river, which has banks to keep it on its course.

It is born and branches into other rivers. It must serve some purpose.

A bad river is one that ends up in a bog.

—Augusto Roa Bastos

The Andes cordillera and Lake Titicaca as seen from the Island of the Sun in Bolivia.

Rigor won't lead you where you want to go, and neither will

asceticism, suffering, or what you think you've understood.

Spice will lead you. The flavor of the loving force.

—A Sierra Grande shaman

On the Day of the Dead, Naney and the inhabitants of Janitzio Island in Mexico visit the *pantéon*, the cemetery, to place flowers on the graves of their loved ones and light candles that burn all night.

Following pages: The church at Mission San Javier—founded in 1749—one of Bolivia's Jesuit missions.

Child with spinning top.

Every time he throws it,

it lands at the very center of the world.

—Octavio Paz

The sun greets the man,

it paints his shadow, in short,

it teaches him what he is.

—Miguel Ángel Asturias

Cabello, a resident of Angahuan, Mexico.

Everything is round.

The constellations are circles of children,

playing at Spy the Earth....

Wheat the torsos of little girls

playing at waving—waving....

The rivers are circles of little boys

playing at crashing in the sea....

The waves are circles of little girls

playing at kissing the ground.

—Gabriela Mistral

A group of schoolchildren in the courtyard of a museum in Morelia, Mexico.

The dawn is replete with fruit; day and night, reconciled, flow like a calm river,

day and night in a long caress like a man and woman in love,

like a single endless river under the vaults of centuries, where the seasons and people flow

toward the living center of origin, beyond end and beginning.

—Octavio Paz

On the Caribbean coast of Mexico sit the Mayan ruins of the important Tulum archaeological site.

Come voices and wings,

come dreams and scents,

come rain, come flowers,

We are all going to sow the seed of life.

—Apolonio Bartolo Ronquillo

On the Rio Bobonaza in the Amazon rain forest of Ecuador.

My kiss goes soaked in the substance

of the earth that I love and journey

with all the roads of my blood

in their sheaths of salty splendor.

—Pablo Neruda

At the market in San Francisco el Alto, Guatemala.

Day, *round day!*

Luminous orange in twenty-four segments,

all transfixed by the same yellow sweetness.

—Octavio Paz

Llamas grazing at the foot of the Altiplano on the edge of Uyuni, Bolivia.
Following pages: The moon rising above Salar de Uyuni.

May 13

How can we afflict ourselves

With the ephemeral,

When, millions and millions of years ago,

In outer space,

Began the ballet of the stars?

—Dom Hélder Câmara

I declare

That you, to live, must arm yourselves with eyes

from head to foot....

Eyes in your arms, to gauge your abilities.

Eyes in your tongue, to think of what you will say.

Eyes in your chest, to help you develop patience.

Eyes in your heart to protect you from first impressions.

Eyes in your very eyes, to see the way that they see.

—Baltasar Gracián

An old regular smokes his cigar in Havana, Cuba.

To become aware of our history is to become aware of our singularity.

It is a moment of reflective repose before we devote ourselves to action again.

—Octavio Paz

Body of light filtered through an agate,

legs of light, belly of light, bays,

solar rock, cloud-colored body,

color of a quick and leaping day,

the hour glitters and becomes a body,

the world is now visible in your body,

it is transparent in your transparency.

—Octavio Paz

Children playing near a fountain in the Pelourinho quarter of Salvador da Bahia, Brazil.

Water bathed me and raised desire

like a branch, my song sustains me

like a wrinkled trunk, with certain scars.

—Pablo Neruda

On the east coast of Santa Maria, Cuba.

There is no unassailable solitude.

All roads lead to the same point:

to the communication of who we are.

And we must travel across lonely and rugged terrain,

through isolation and silence, to reach the magic zone

where we can dance an awkward dance or sing a melancholy song;

but in the dance and the song are consummated the most ancient rituals of awareness—

the awareness of being men, and of believing in common destiny.

—Pablo Neruda

A village in the Tarabuco Valley, Bolivia.

Humankind has perhaps a hundred senses,

of which the five we know disappear at death.

But the ninety-five others remain alive.

—José Balza

A baby enjoys a nap in the Amazon rain forest, Ecuador.
Following pages: In a park in Antigua, Guatemala.

May 20

Life. Survival. Life—hot, ardent, imposing.

The mystery reclaimed.

To live is to bring back the mystery of life.

—Miguel Ángel Asturias

Artistic sensibility is the capacity to make the invisible visible by

embracing the marginal, the perverse, the excluded.

—Carlos Fuentes

Inside an old colonial home in Cartagena's old city, Colombia.

A *revolutionary is not born in a just world.*

He *is born in a painful world.*

—Rigoberta Menchú

There is no motion, feeling, or idea that is not created or propelled by death's

vital passion: infinite love of life and its goodness. When for reasons of inertia,

fatigue, or mere forgetfulness I disregard my passion, I am really dead.

—Luis Cardoza y Aragón

Children play in the church at Mission Concepción, one of Bolivia's Jesuit missions, founded in 1704.

Yet my slings are whirling. I am here, I scream, desire.

My strength and my pain, in the night. I want it.

My strength is my pain, in the night. I want it.

I must open this door. And go through it. I must defeat it.

My stones must reach their target. I scream. Cry. Desire.

—Pablo Neruda

An old sea lion on North Seymour Island in the Galápagos, Ecuador.

Poetry does not attempt to console man facing death, but to allow him

to see that life and death are inseparable; that they are all.

—Octavio Paz

In Mexico on the Day of the Dead, families decorate the cemetery with flowers and spend
all day and night celebrating with their dead.

I *am one of those people who will dive into the swell, ready to face terrible dangers,*

to catch a starfish or a sunfish and feel the joy of being alive.

—Francisco Coloane

Playing on the dike in the port of Salvador da Bahia, Brazil.
Following pages: A chapel towers over the Colca Valley of Peru and the deepest canyon in the world.

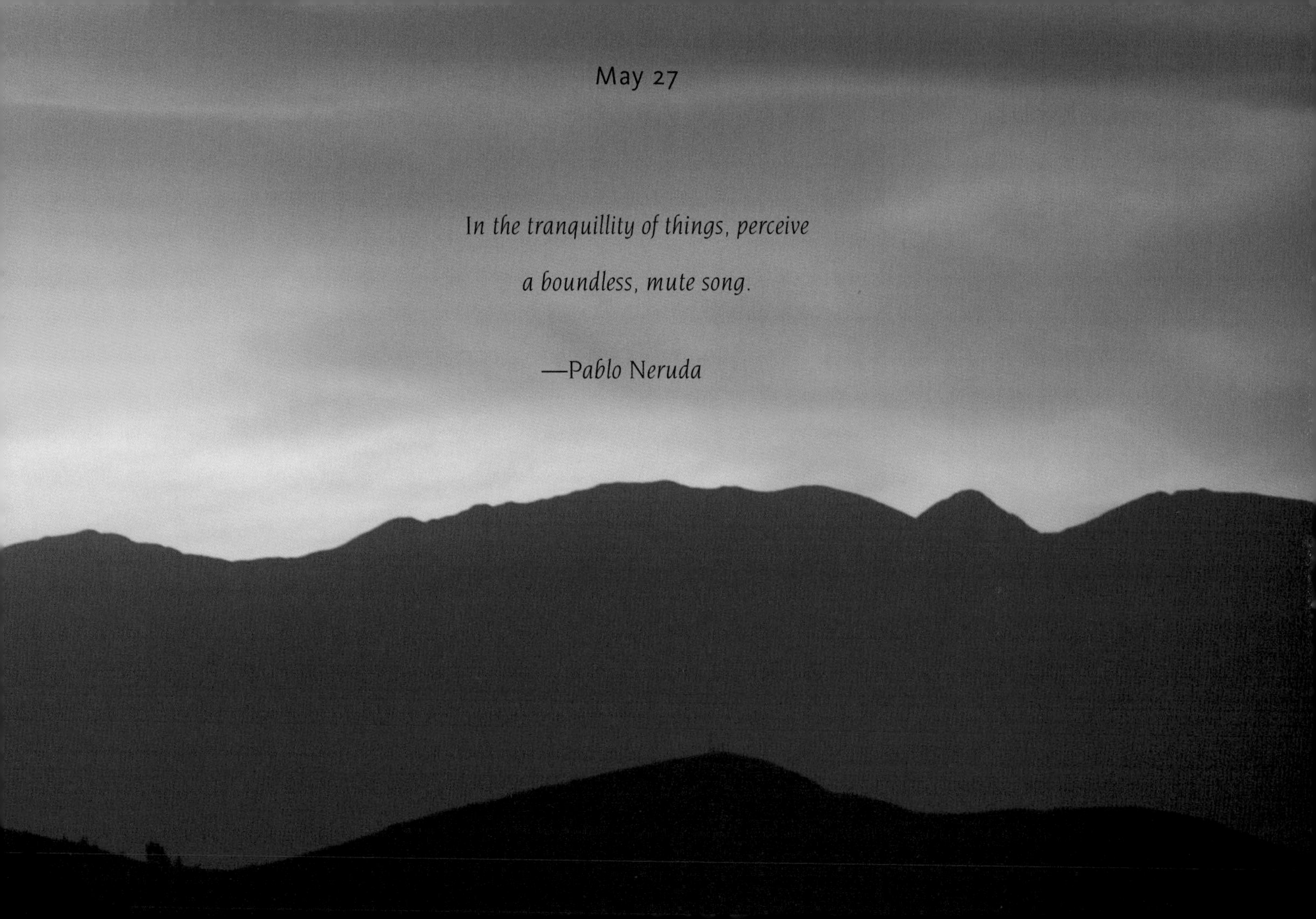

May 27

In the tranquillity of things, perceive

a boundless, mute song.

—Pablo Neruda

Ask your body.

The greater the refusal, the more intense the pain.

—Amazonian oral tradition

A child reluctant to be treated by the healer in Sarayaku.

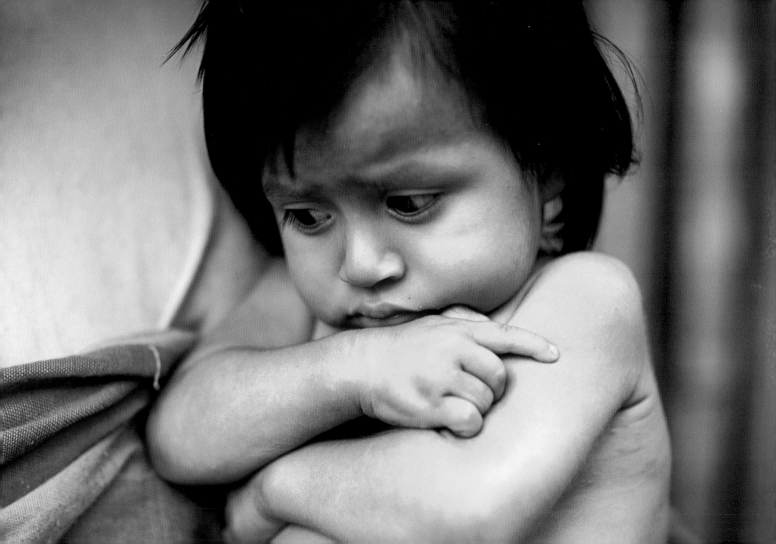

The most fleeting thought obeys an invisible plan,

and may crown, or inaugurate, a secret design.

—Jorge Luis Borges

A girl wearing traditional clothes in the Colca Valley of Peru.

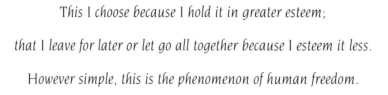

This I choose because I hold it in greater esteem;

that I leave for later or let go all together because I esteem it less.

However simple, this is the phenomenon of human freedom.

—Enrique Dussel

In the alleys of the village of Todos Santos, Guatemala.

Let us evade death in gentle phases,

remembering always that being alive demands

a greater effort than the simple act of breathing.

Ardent patience alone will empower us

to win a splendid happiness.

—Pablo Neruda

The ritual drink of chicha, a fermented maize beverage, as practiced in the community of Sarayaku, deep in Ecuador's Amazon.

I attested to the world: I confessed the strangeness of the world.

I sang the eternal: the return of moonlight and cheeks enticing love.

I commemorated in verse the city that surrounds me, the tortured suburbs.

I launched my psalms to the rooftop horizon, and they came back with a taste for far-off lands.

I spoke of surprise where others speak only of habit.

—Jorge Luis Borges

Two-year-old Jimena, the daughter of miners in the Cerro Rico mine in Potosí, Bolivia.

Every city is an epic, a saga,

A constructed, painted, and sculpted "Popol Vuh."

A poem in stone.

—Luis Cardoza y Aragón

The capital city of La Paz, Bolivia, 12,100 feet (3,700 m) above sea level.
Following pages: On the streets of Antigua, Guatemala.

If we do not recognize our humanity in others,

we shall not recognize it in ourselves.

—Carlos Fuentes

Each individual, each thing, each instant:

a unique, incomparable, incommensurable reality.

—Octavio Paz

Twelve-year-old Jesus Omar, an Aymara Indian, on Anapi Island on Lake Titicaca, Peru.

At night if I'm feeling sad

I go out for a walk

on the great plains of the sky.

My heart wakes up

covered with dew.

—Humberto Ak'Abal

After one of the frequent rainstorms in the San Rafael Lagoon, Chile.

June 6

You couldn't see that life is only given to those who cry,

to those who love, and have loved.

And if you refuse yourself to passion, you will lose yourself to madness.

—Vinícius de Moraes

Bearing a statue of Jesus carrying the cross during Holy Week in Antigua, Guatemala.

Like the moon

behind the eucalypti,

elegant and beautiful,

so was she,

humble, simple, reserved,

barefoot like my sadness.

Her eyes, tiny kernels of black corn.

Morning brought her,

the night took her away.

Heaven, too,

fell in love with her.

—Humberto Ak'Abal

Wearing festive makeup at the children's carnival in Salvador da Bahia, Brazil.

June 8

Our deaths illuminate our lives.

If our deaths lack meaning, our lives also lacked it.

—Octavio Paz

Decorating graves with flowers on the Day of the Dead in Mexico.

My spirit is all harmony and rhythm:

everything in my being is music and song,

from the saddest requiem of tears

to the triumphal melody of joy.

—Oral tradition

Luis Rocha, violinist and director of the church at Mission Santa Ana, one of Bolivia's Jesuit missions.

June 10

Each day you are different:

in memory, actuality, and hope.

The same, as usual, never.

—Luis Cardoza y Aragón

A girl on the Island of Janitzio on Lake Pátzcuaro, Mexico.

Make of your life

a bell that rings or a furrow in which

the glowing tree of ideas flowers and bears fruit.

—Nicolas Guillén

The entrance to the cemetery in Janitzio on Lake Pátzcuaro, Mexico.

The adolescent is also ignorant of the future changes that will affect the countenance

he sees in the water. The mask of an old man is as indecipherable at first glance as

a sacred stone covered with occult symbols: it is the history of various amorphous features

that only take shape, slowly and vaguely, after the profoundest contemplation.

Eventually these features are seen as a face, and later as a mask, a meaning, a history.

—Octavio Paz

A child on the Altiplano of Bolivia.

June 13

Man dreams the dream of things;

time thinks the dreams of men.

—Octavio Paz

An old woman at the foot of an Inca wall in the old city of Cuzco, Peru.

Each time we affirm one part of us, we deny another.

—Octavio Paz

A fruit vendor in the old city of Antigua, Guatemala.

There are many ways of lying, but the most repugnant one is to speak the truth, all of the truth, while hiding the spirit of things.

—Juan Carlos Onetti

A young man belonging to the Sarayaku community in the Amazon rain forest of Ecuador.

Every human creature harbors two souls. One looks from the inside out,

the other from the outside in.... Naturally, he who loses

one of these two halves loses one half of his existence.

—J. M. Machado de Assis

Seven-year-old Mery, whose parents are miners in the Cerro Rico mine in Potosí, Bolivia.
Following pages: A young Sarayoku man gathers fruit from trees in the Amazon rain forest of Ecuador.

June 17

By day, it's man
and jungle.
By night, man is jungle.

—Luis Sepúlveda

To hear

thoughts,

see

what we say,

touch

the body of an idea.

Eyes close,

the words open.

—Octavio Paz

The glass canopy of the Gran Hotel in Mexico City dates back to the colonial era.

June 19

Between what I see and what I say,

between what I say and what I keep silent,

between what I keep silent and what I dream,

between what I dream and what I forget:

poetry.

It slips

—Octavio Paz

A young student in Havana, Cuba, celebrates the anniversary of the birth of poet José Martí.

Every moment he must remake, re-create, modify the personage he is playing,

until at last the moment arrives when reality

and appearance, the lie and the truth, are one.

—Octavio Paz

Performers in the Ballet Folklórico of Mexico at the Palace of Fine Arts in Mexico City.

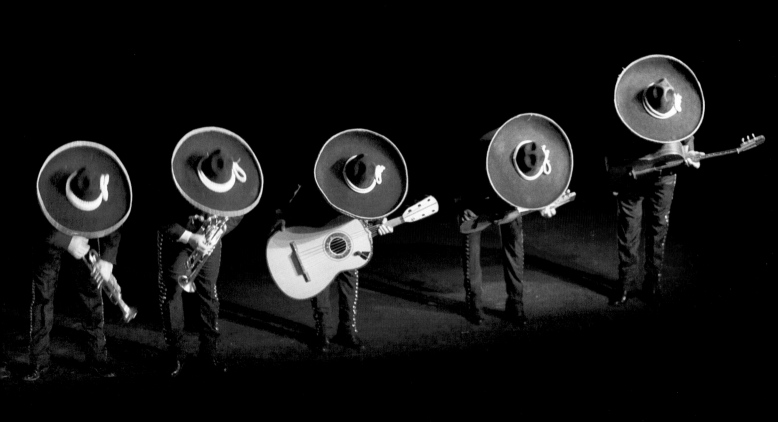

Only because

I err

do I get it right:

I create

Myself.

Margin of error:

margin of liberty.

—Orides Fontela

Francisco Peisej, eleven years old, a young boatman in Santa Cruz de la Laguna, Guatemala.

June 22

The deeper we burrow into our soil, the more we renew ourselves....

the more we are local, the more we are likely to rise to the forefront of the universal.

—Pablo Neruda

Cultivation of potatoes on Anapia Island on Lake Titicaca, Peru.

To be original implies departing from yourself,

from what you are, from your own reality.

—Leopoldo Zéa

A schoolchild in Havana, Cuba, celebrating the anniversary of the birth of poet José Martí.
Following pages: A llama rejoins its herd on the Bolivian Altiplano.

June 24

While we sleep here, elsewhere we are awake.

Thus each person is two people.

—Jorge Luis Borges

How do we become conceited

with our social status,

with our position,

with our shine,

if the stars are immense

and seem like light drops?

—Dom Hélder Câmara

The entrance to the capitol building in Havana, Cuba.

June 26

The only treasure that survives after death is all that we have given.

—Aymara oral tradition

The market in Solola, Guatemala.

We suffer because we believe we give more than we receive.

—Niña Mari, a Maya Quitché Indian

Cultivation in the fertile valley of Fuentes Georginas, Guatemala.

The Soul of the World is nourished by people's happiness.

—*Paulo Coelho*

Luzmila and Maria on Anapia Island, the home of Aymara communities in Peru.

Make me opulent in giving,

so I can be as fecund as you are,

make my heart and thought

as vast as the world!

—Gabriela Mistral

On the Rio Bobonaza in the Amazon rain forest of Ecuador.

He who is Indian knows very well what it means to be from here, to be from America:

first tickling of tears and the breeze, battle against fangs in the muzzle of doubt,

unbridled force that erupts and surges forward, molded out of all that breathes and tires

and leads to the prophetic kindness of Man

who, watching, averts his eyes, who, listening, averts his ears

and, surprised by his senses, rises from his mute entrails

to the secret suave banks of the water lying in his breath.

—Miguel Ángel Asturias

A woman from the countryside arriving at the market in Tarabuco, Bolivia, to sell her crafts.
Following pages: At the entrance to the church of Zunil, Guatemala.

Any life, however long and complicated it may be, actually consists of a single moment—the moment when we know forevermore who we are.

—Jorge Luis Borges

When I *bite into a fruit, you will know its delights.*

—*Pablo Neruda*

In a valley near Tarabuco, Bolivia, young villagers sing songs of seduction during the annual Phujllay festival.

I *embrace joy in the form of the moment,*

your body.

—Fabricio Estrada

A carnival parade in Salvador da Bahia, Brazil.

The new language. I speak it.

Not with my fingers. I speak it with my eyelids. It is the eyes.

The new language is a blinking of the eyes.

To create the fiction, the reflection, the movement by blinking.

To translate the language of solid clay forms

and the melody of pebbles into words-reflected-in-the-water, songs of fictive images.

Other beauty. Another sign. Language of the eyes. Moving your lips is useless.

—Miguel Ángel Asturias

A village child in the Atacama desert, Chile.

Words

are only good to play with

and to make poems.

—Magdalena Thompson

Three-year-old Naicer and his brother at the market in Otavalo, Ecuador.

"Mestizo, mestizo!"

The sun has already asked the moon

to swap shifts

so that it can see you go by…

—Nahua oral tradition

Sunset on the Bolivian Altiplano, 13,100 feet (4,000 m) above sea level.

Such is the virtue of black blood: where one drop falls, everything blooms.

—Thilda Herbillon-Moubayed

During carnival in Salvador da Bahia, Brazil.
Following pages: Early morning on Guatemala's Lake Atitlán.

July 8

Deep inside the human soul,

in its deepest recesses,

lies the secret of resurrection.

It must be excavated.

—Octavio Paz

Thanks be to life that gave me so much.

It gave me hearing, with my ears wide open,

Recording crickets and canaries night and day;

Hammers, turbines, barks, storms,

And the tender voice of my beloved.

Thanks be to life that gave me so much.

—Violeta Parra

A home in the old colonial quarter of Cartagena, Colombia.

To live is to be separated from what we were

in order to approach what we are going to be in the mysterious future.

Solitude is the profoundest fact of the human condition.

Man is the only being who knows he is alone, and the only one who seeks out another.

—Octavio Paz

Built 12,500 feet (3,800 m) above sea level, Pontarema's church stands between Salar de Coipasa and Salar de Uyuni, Bolivia.

Love is one of the clearest examples of that double instinct

which causes us to dig deeper into our own selves

and, at the same time, to emerge from ourselves and to realize ourselves in another:

death and re-creation, solitude and communion.

—Octavio Paz

Amorous sea lions on Floreana Island in the Galápagos, Ecuador.

The human mind always harbors a battle between antagonistic forces.

When one of these forces seems to triumph, the other draws into itself

and, sooner or later, leaps back more vigorous than ever.

—Jorge Luis Borges

A caravan of llamas crosses a pass 15,090 feet (4,600 m) above sea level in the Cordillera Apolobamba, Bolivia.

The feeling that we are alone has a double significance:

on the one hand it is self-awareness,

and on the other it is a longing to escape from ourselves.

—Octavio Paz

A dancer in the Ballet Folklórico of Mexico performs at the Palace of Fine Arts in Mexico City.

July 14

Perhaps, then, I won't know how to appreciate your caresses,

because your being has melted into my veins.

—Pablo Neruda

July 15

Human beings are both free and dependent.

They are the very seat of ambivalence.

They want to be chained and unchained.

And they want to chain and unchain.

—Thilda Herbillon-Moubayed

I had another name

when the song turned to water in the river.

And I had another river when the jaguar in me

sang on the riverbank.

—Humberto Ak'Abal

Child from a village in the Atacama desert of Chile.

Love is not in the other, it is in you.

—Niña Mari, a Maya Quitché Indian

In the courtyard of an old colonial home in Antigua, Guatemala.

To love is two,

always two,

embrace and struggle,

two is the longing to be one,

and to be the other, male or female,

two knows no rest,

it is never complete,

it whirls

around its own shadow,

searching

for what we lost at birth.

—Octavio Paz

A walk through the village of Todos Santos, Guatemala.

We are suspended between solitude and fraternity.

Each one of our actions aims to end our isolation—our state of being orphaned—

and to restore, however precariously, our union with the world and the other.

—Octavio Paz

A beach in Cayo Santa Maria, Cuba.

How well they know the rhythm, what elegance,

What style! What a figure!

What bearing! What arrogance!

What distinguished dancing.

This is how you dance the tango,

I make an eight;

for these arabesques, I am like the painter,

now a bullfight, once around, sitting.

What is at stake in the tango is both a personal

and a shared destiny,

impossible to control.

—Argentine song

In shadow, two dancers in Antigua, Guatemala.

Music, states of felicity, mythology, faces marked by time,

certain twilights, and certain places wish to tell us something,

or told us something we should not have lost, or are on the verge of telling us;

this imminence of a revelation that does not take place is, perhaps, the aesthetic fact.

—Jorge Luis Borges

Relics of Olmec civilization in La Venta Park in Villahermosa, Mexico.
Following pages: The rainy season at Bolivia's Salar de Uyuni.

In every mirror lurks a double,

an adversary who reflects and humiliates us.

—Octavio Paz

Bless thirst

for teaching us the purity of water.

Bless thirst

for bringing us together

around the fountain.

—Orides Fontela

The Rio Bobonaza in Ecuador's Amazon region.

July 24

To exist is to live together, to live with others.

A *person's* conscience makes living with others possible.

—Niña Mari, a Maya Quitché Indian

Market day in Quetzaltenango, Guatemala.

All of you, O my friends!

You know it and I know it:

our life passes at once,

in a single day, in a single night,

nothingness.

We came only to meet each other.

On Earth, life is but a loan.

—POPOL VUH, *Mayan sacred text*

On the Day of the Dead in Mexico, families visit the cemetery to decorate the graves of their loved ones.

What's behind that door?

Don't knock, don't ask, no one answers,

nothing can open it,

not the picklock of curiosity

nor the little key of reason,

nor the hammer of impatience.

Don't talk, don't ask,

come closer, put your ear to it,

can't you hear it breathing?

There, on the other side,

someone like you asks:

what's behind that door?

—Octavio Paz

At the entrance to the church in Yanque in the Colca Valley of Peru.

If you look closely at the truths that most resemble the truth, if you weigh them,

you will see that they are only half-truths or not true at all.

—Mario Vargas Llosa

Twilight embraces the cacti of the Bolivian Altiplano.

Our solitude has the same roots as religious feelings.

It is a form of orphanhood,

an obscure awareness that we have been torn from the All, and an ardent search:

a flight and a return, an effort to re-establish the bonds that unite us with the universe.

—Octavio Paz

Sunday Mass at the Mission of San Miguel, one of the Jesuit missions founded in 1721 in Bolivia.

Following pages: On the Peruvian Altiplano, in the shadow of the majestic Misti volcano, a ninety-year-old man searches for brush to light his kitchen fire.

July 29

Traveling leads you to encounter the other, which will always be a way of encountering yourself.

—Luis Sepúlveda

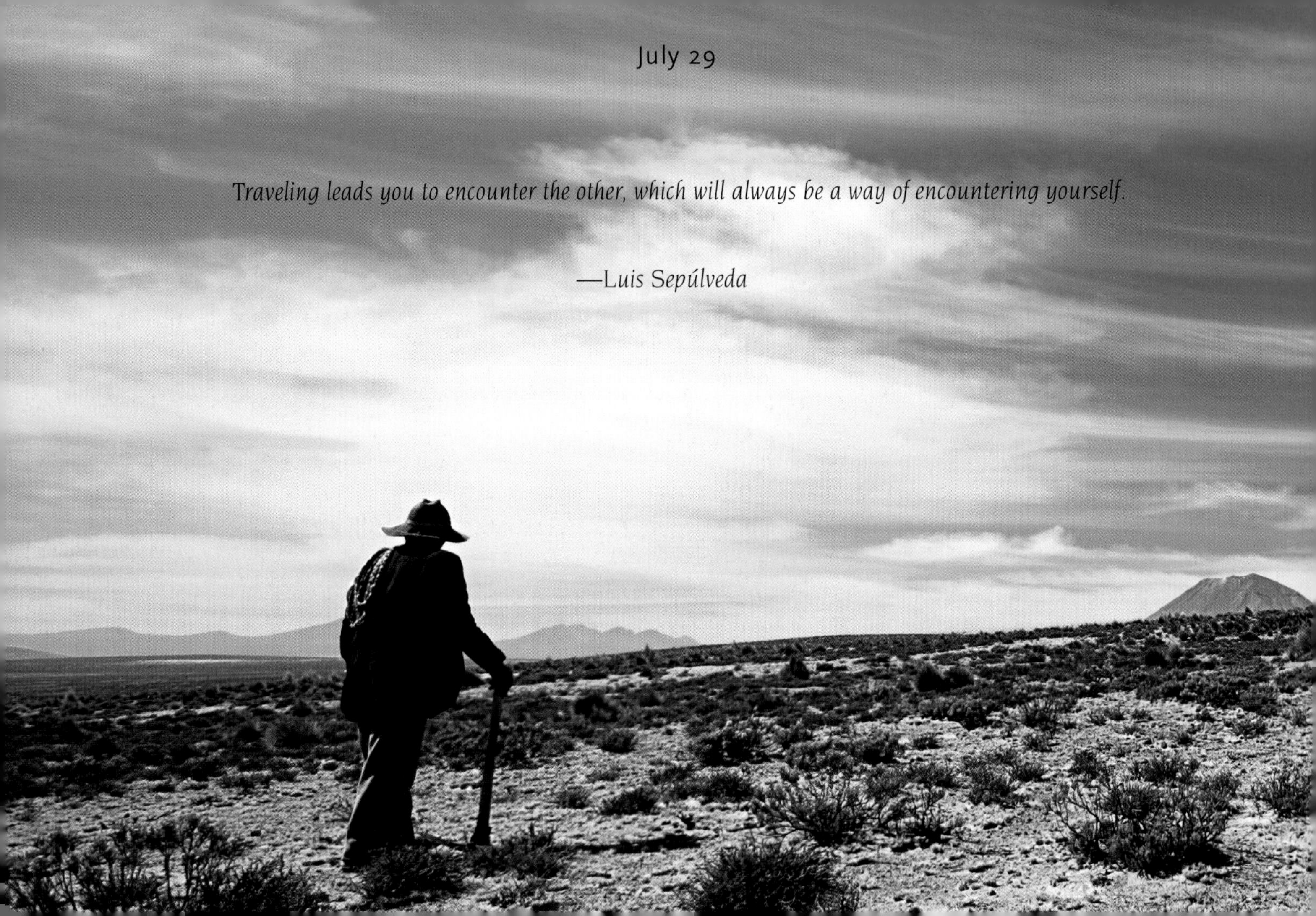

Poetry

says

What I keep silent,

keeps silent

what I say,

dreams

what I forget.

—Octavio Paz

A tradeswoman in Otavalo, Ecuador, wearing the typical local necklace.

The lover seeks his lost identity in the beloved.

—Octavio Paz

Tropical flora in Antigua, Guatemala.

How do I understand that I am what I am only because

another person sees me or completes me?

—Carlos Fuentes

Applying festive makeup for the children's carnival in Salvador da Bahia, Brazil.

Between the one who receives and the one who gives,

between the one who speaks and the one who listens,

there is an inconsolable eternity.

The poet knows this.

—Roberto Juarroz

A shepherdess on the road to Salar de Coipasa, Bolivia.

My humanity is to feel that we are the voices of the same misery....

My name is someone and anyone.

I believe that my days and nights

match in poverty and in wealth the days of God and all men.

—Jorge Luis Borges

Religious rites during Holy Week in Antigua, Guatemala.

Do not fear me, do not fall

into your rancor again.

Shake off my word that came to wound you

and let it fly through the open window.

—Pablo Neruda

A villager and her eagle in Yanque in the Colca Valley, Peru.
Following pages: Nora Delgado Vega stands at Bolivia's Salar de Uyuni, the largest salt flat in the world.

August 5

You have made me indestructible because, with you,

I do not end in myself.

—Pablo Neruda

With you I learned

To see the light on the other side of the moon.

With you I learned

That your presence cannot be replaced so soon.

I learned that a kiss can be softer and deeper,

That I could be taken from this world tomorrow.

The beautiful things, I lived them with you,

And also I learned

That I was born the day that I met you.

—Armando Manzanero

Claudia Lucia Diaz Lopez, a dancer from Antigua, Guatemala.

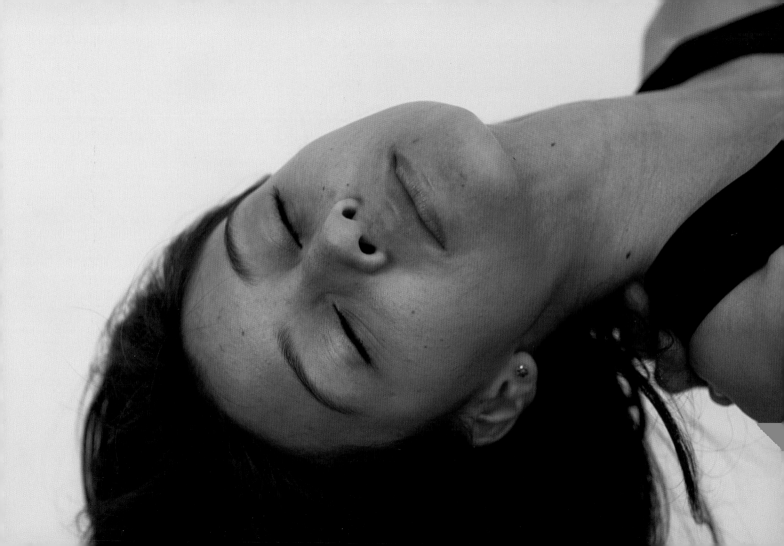

José, leaning on his polyglot stick, a shepherd of images, showed me some poor

lion's-heart cement and said: a bridge, a great bridge, we just don't see it.

Since that day, I have crossed bridges that stretch from here to there,

from never to always, since that day, engineer of thin air,

I have been building the interminable bridge between the inaudible and the invisible.

—Octavio Paz

Sunday mass at the church in San Andrès Xecul, Guatemala.

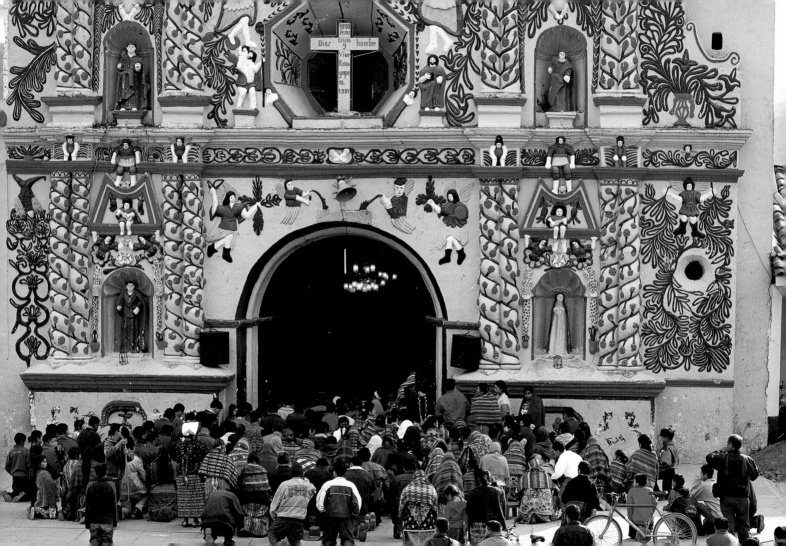

Thanks be to life that gave me so much.

It gave me a voice and letters

With which to think words and say:

Mother, friend, light that illuminates

The path to the soul that I love

Thanks be to life that gave me so much.

—Violeta Parra

An embrace on the beach in Salvador da Bahia, Brazil.

Love is not a "natural" thing.

It is something human, the most human trait of all.

Something that we have made ourselves

and that is not found in nature.

—Octavio Paz

Passing by the Jesuit mission in the village of Concepción, Bolivia.

Pleasure wounds,

the wound flowers.

In the garden of caresses

I clipped the flower of blood

to adorn your hair.

The flower became a word.

—Octavio Paz

In a valley near Tarabuco, Bolivia, a young villager in holiday costume for the annual Phujllay festival.

Love me, you, smile at me,

help me to be good.

Do not wound yourself in me, for it will be useless,

do not wound me because you wound yourself.

—Pablo Neruda

The market in Chivay, in the Colca Valley of Peru.
Following pages: Near Española Island in the Galápagos, Ecuador.

August 12

The essential qualities of love are receptivity and reciprocity:

I open myself and you open yourself and away we go.

—Mario Vargas Llosa

Flower that speaks the song of life

and is grace and perfect delight.

I almost envy your splendor,

I, the root, sunken in time.

You are the reality; I the hope.

You the rarefied summit; I the passageway.

The sap of my tears overtakes you

and I pardon your light, because I love you.

—Serafín Quiteño

In Guatemala's virgin rain forest.

As humans, all of us will try to engage in the existence of others

or to make others engage in our own existence. But this engagement

leads to the greatest difficulties, for we will always be more

inclined to impose our existence than to accept the existence of others.

—Leopoldo Zea

The plaza de Armas, the central square in Cuzco, Peru, former capital of the Inca Empire.

I *must have been looking for something in you*

something of me that is in you

and that you never have to give me.

—Jaime Sabines

Nora Delgado Vega, twenty-six-years old, in Chivay, her village in the Colca Valley of Peru.

Good for me is the look in your eyes

so warm and steadfast,

and your frank silence

surely is good for me,

good for me is the temperance

of your life,

good for me is your future

that is present freedom

and your constant struggle,

yes, it is certainly good for me,

good for me, too,

is your battle

without medals,

good for me is the modesty

of your reasonable pride,

and your steady hand

is certainly good for me,

good for me is your way,

comrade.

—Mario Benedetti

Raul Santi Aranda, five years old, with his father, from Sarayaku in Ecuador's Amazon region.

Don't try to bring all your brothers into your world....

You would strip them of their difference.

—Niña Mari, a Maya Quitché Indian

In the Amazon rain forest of Ecuador.

Someone is over there, constructing God in the half-light.

A man begets God, creates him…

from the depths of his sickness, of his void,

he continues to build God through words.

—Jorge Luis Borges

The Amazon rain forest of Ecuador bathed in the full moon.
Following pages: A red rock crab on Española Island in the Galápagos, Ecuador.

August 19

If the eye were not solar,

How could it perceive light?

—Homero Aridjis

Aconcagua, stern face,

kissed by the eternal God

and by the last red of sunset.

You hold something in your hands,

that prays for your two people:

Peace among men, peace,

a blessing on the child

being born, a sweetness

for the dying.

—Gabriela Mistral

Crossing the Cordillera Apolobamba in Bolivia.

I don't have to understand the Other to feel solidarity with him,

or to "create with" him. I cannot fathom the Other through intelligence;

our relationship is not based on knowledge but on trusting his word.

The Other is a life and his life's goal. His life and his goal are

revealed to me only because he is willing to reveal them to me.

—Enrique Dussel

An Amazonian parrot in Sarayaku, Ecuador.

If you arrive in a strange land

bow

if the place is bizarre

bow

if the day is utter strangeness

surrender—

you are infinitely more peculiar.

—Orides Fontela

A sea iguana on Española Island in the Galápagos, Ecuador.

Society is the joining of two differences.

—Quechua oral tradition

At the children's carnival in Salvador da Bahia, Brazil.

Nights and oceans divide us,

secular modifications,

no less the bloods, the climates, the empires;

but indecipherably something

joins us together,

the mysterious love of words,

this commerce of sounds and symbols.

—Jorge Luis Borges

Remains of the Mayan city of Toninà, Mexico.

We are like the birds:

as you know, birds change feathers according to the seasons.

But we can tell the difference between the song of a sparrow and that of a dove:

the song continues.

—Aymara oral tradition

A frigate bird in the Galápagos Islands, Ecuador.
Following pages: The San Pedro and Tolimán volcanoes flank the shores of Guatemala's Lake Atitlán.

August 26

And my little boat will carry me to your dream.

—Gabriel García Márquez

In the Quitché language

We do not say "adiós"

but "katinch'ab'ej chik"

(I'll talk to you again).

—Humberto Ak'Abal

At the market in San Francisco el Alto, Guatemala.

I want to be Water

to bathe my skin in your fate.

To be Air,

to hang on to the last sigh.

To be Fire,

to embrace your velvet skin.

To be Earth,

to return to the beginning,

at the end of our encounter.

—Roberto Reséndiz Carmona

Harvested on Lake Titicaca in Peru, the *llachu* plant is used as fodder for cows.

The sun greets the fish,

he teaches him how he is,

he tells the chirping bird:

"Don't take yourself for a flower,"

the bird knows,

but isn't it possible to dream?

In dreams to be a flower or a boat.

—Miguel Ángel Asturias

Fishermen set out at dawn from Lake Titicaca's Anapia Island, in Peru.

The path of the Indian transforms

pride into humility,

greed into frugality,

lust into detachment

toward purity of heart.

—Maya Quitché oral tradition

An assembly of the Raqchi community on Peru's Altiplano.

We glorify things with the lie of evanescent beauty

in order to escape the truth of eternal beauty.

And not only the clay lied.

The gold, silver, jade, rich feathers, accomplices of the sun,

helped to create this universe of appearances.

But all that came to an end with the sun.

—Miguel Ángel Asturias

Important archaeological remains at the Mayan ceremonial center in Palenque, Mexico.

September 1

We must learn to topple the idols,

sex, car, bank account,

pride, domination,

through asceticism,

throw out the superfluous.

Learn to be light as air, dreams set free.

—Octavio Paz

On the streets of downtown Mexico City, Mexico.

Following pages: A young violinist plays in the Jesuit Mission of San Miguel de Velasco in Bolivia.

September 2

A grain of poetry is enough to flavor an entire century.

—José Martí

September 3

If we tear off these masks, if we open ourselves up, if—in brief—

we face our own selves, then we can truly begin to live and to think.

Nakedness and defenselessness are awaiting us.

But there, in that "open" solitude, transcendence is also waiting:

the outstretched hands of other solitary beings.

—Octavio Paz

At the Sunday market in Tarabuco, Bolivia.

To hold out your hand,

soft as a kiss,

passionate,

this is how the ages and epochs began.

—Niña Mari, a Maya Quitché Indian

The unspoken bond between a mother and daughter in Antigua, Guatemala.

No culture ever developed, bloomed, and matured without feeding on other cultures and,

in turn, nourishing others through a continuous process of borrowing and giving,

reciprocal influences and intermingling. Any attempt to determine what

belonged to which culture would be entirely arbitrary.

—Mario Vargas Llosa

A village in the Bolivian Altiplano, 13,780 feet (4,200 m) above sea level.

Those people suffering, who are they?

I don't know, but they are my people.

—Pablo Neruda

Tomas Mayo Vargas, a twelve-year-old orphan, after a day's work in the Cerro Rico mine in Potosí, Bolivia.

Every culture is born of the mixture of encounter, of shocks.

On the contrary, it is isolation that kills civilizations.

—Octavio Paz

Public buses and barouches on the streets of Havana, Cuba.

Between individuals as between nations, peace is respect for the rights of others.

—Benito Juárez

Shining shoes on the main plaza of Xela, Guatemala.
Following pages: The market in Solola, Guatemala.

September 9

Better than bread is its sharing, its division.

—Dom Hélder Câmara

I *exist through your eyes.*

—*Latin American oral tradition*

On November 1, the day of *angelitos*, or little angels,
Purépecha children on Janitzio Island in Mexico take offerings to the cemetery.

May what your eyes see stay in your heart.

—Aymara oral tradition

A girl in the alleys of Salvador da Bahia's old city in Brazil.

Your cathedral heart covers us in this instant, like the firmament,

and your great grandiose song, your volcanic tenderness,

fills all the heights like a burning statue.

—Pablo Neruda

Frescoes in the convent of San Nicolàs Tolentino, founded in 1548, in Actopan, Mexico.

Your breast is enough for my heart,

and my wings for your freedom.

What was sleeping above your soul will rise

out of my mouth to heaven.

—Pablo Neruda

In the market in San Francisco el Alto, Guatemala.

If your path has no heart,

leave it.

—Amazonian oral tradition

The church at the San Miguel Jesuit mission, founded in 1721 in Bolivia.

May my heart forever be the embers of your censer.

—Luis Cardoza y Aragón

On the beach in Salvador da Bahia, Brazil.
Following pages: Sunset on North Seymour Island in the Galápagos, Ecuador.

September 16

Poetry is memory bathed in tears.

—Miguel Ángel Asturias

No one is someone; a single immortal man is all men.

—Jorge Luis Borges

Stone relief panel at the National Museum of Anthropology in Mexico City.

We should begin by ensuring that every child in the world is able to

eat and go to school. Let us internationalize children, no matter where they are born,

by treating them as a world heritage deserving of the entire world's attention.

—Cristovam Buarque

Freshly scolded by his mother at the market in Chivay, Peru.

If I feed the poor, I am called a saint.

If I ask why the poor are hungry, I am called a Communist.

—Dom Hélder Câmara

Detail of a religious statue in Antigua, Guatemala.

I write for the people even though they cannot

read my poetry with their rural eyes.

The moment will come when a line, the air

that turns my life upside down, will reach their ears....

That is all I need, the only crown I desire.

—Pablo Neruda

In the mountainous region of Sucre, Bolivia.

In this world, we are all equal!

Hey! Equal to whom?

—Latin American oral tradition

A tired miner after a day deep in the Cerro Rico mine in Potosí, Bolivia.

Lord of the Cacao

We ask you to help us never to lack work or health

so that we can build a place fit to live in,

where faith, hope, and love will never be lacking.

—Prayer posted in the Mexico City Cathedral

Statue of Christ in the church of Actopan, Mexico.

We will share only

what goes on

within us:

simplicity

struggle

hope.

We will share only

this greatest intensity:

absolute speech

that belongs completely to us.

We will share only

the unified bread

and the faceless water.

—Orides Fontela

Family life in a hut in Sarayaku, Ecuador.
Following pages: Tobacco fields in the Viñales Valley, Cuba.

I *ask you, can there be a community without sharing?*

To pass on and to share, that is how we are eternal.

—Aymara oral tradition

A *driver comes to a garage.*

"*I want my horn changed. Fix it so it makes four or five very loud blasts.*"

"*Why do you want such a loud horn?*"

"*Because I have no brakes.*"

—Latin American oral tradition

A makeshift repair job in the streets of Havana, Cuba.

If not for the sun,

the poor would have

long since frozen to death.

They die of hunger

little by little.

—Humberto Ak'Abal

A sea lion at sunset on North Seymour Island in the Galápagos, Ecuador.

There is no me, we are always us,

the others.

—Octavio Paz

A festive crowd at carnival in Salvador da Bahia, Brazil.

Looking at this necklace as beautiful as a dream,

I especially admired the thread linking the stones

that sacrificed itself to anonymity so all could be as one.

—Dom Hélder Câmara

Jewelry of a young Amazonian Indian, Brazil.

Integration has never happened through self-interest and money,

but through the thread of culture, through that dense tissue

of strands joined together by shared values.

—Federico Mayor

At the market in San Francisco el Alto, Guatemala.

We are Indian, black, European, but above all mixed, "mestizo."

We are Iberian and Greek, Roman and Jewish, Arab, Gothic, and Gypsy.

Spain and the New World are centers where multiple

cultures meet—centers of incorporation, not of exclusion.

When we exclude, we betray ourselves. When we include, we find ourselves.

—Carlos Fuentes

View of roots in a Rio de Janeiro park, Brazil.
Following pages: An isolated church in the Colca Valley of Peru.

The divine is in the human.

—José Martí

Perhaps to love is to learn

to walk through this world.

To learn to be silent

like the oak and the linden of the fable.

To learn to see.

Your glance scatters seeds.

It planted a tree.

I talk

because you shake its leaves.

—Octavio Paz

In the Petén rain forest of Guatemala.

October 3

The true revolution must begin inside each of us.

—*Che Guevara*

A farm woman in the market of Tarabuco, Bolivia.

Evil is not just a metaphysical or religious notion:

it is a sensuous, biological, psychological, and historical reality.

Evil can be touched,

evil hurts.

—Octavio Paz

A red rock crab on North Seymour Island in the Galápagos, Ecuador.

Are we evil?

Or is evil outside us, and we its instrument, its tool?

Evil is dehumanization.

—Octavio Paz

On the streets of Havana, Cuba.

Moderation consists in accepting the relativity of values and

political and historical acts, on condition that this relativity is inserted

into a vision of the whole of human destiny on Earth.

—Octavio Paz

The salt marshes of the Urubamba Valley have been in use since the days when the Incas ruled Peru.

Happy is the one who understands the necessity of changing to remain always oneself.

—Dom Hélder Câmara

A young girl in Sarayaku, Ecuador, creates traditional face paintings.

Following pages: Icebergs that have broken away from San Rafael glacier in Patagonia, Chile. The ice floe in the foreground is about 33 feet (10 m) long.

To fight evil is to fight ourselves.

And that is the meaning of history.

—Octavio Paz

When a fish is in the ocean, the ocean is infinite.

When a bird is in the sky, the sky is infinite.

—Kouma (Caribbean) oral tradition

The sun sets on North Seymour Island in the Galápagos, Ecuador.

Only out of doubt and conflict can any harmony ever rise.

And what greater conflict is there than that between nature and civilization,

dream and reality?

—Carlos Fuentes

Fishermen on Lake Pátzcuaro in Mexico.

Once upon a time in a distant land, there was a black sheep.

He was executed by a firing squad.

A century later, the repentant herd erected an equestrian statue that fit well in the park.

Henceforth, each time black sheep appeared they were rapidly placed before a firing squad

so that ordinary sheep of future generations could also practice their sculpture.

—Augusto Monterroso

The crown of a tower of the capitol in Havana, Cuba.

Your name, they say, is "Flower heart who follows woman and sun."

Also "Liana hair," when you fall into the cloud of dream.

I call you what I always called you:

servant, laborer, serf, caretaker, Indian.

—Miguel Ángel Asturias

Farmers returning from the fields in the Sacred Valley of Peru.

God has not created the world yet: he is only imagining it, as if in a dream.

This is why the world is perfect but chaotic.

—Augusto Monterroso

A young girl helps her mother at the market in Solola, Guatemala.

When temporal or spiritual authorities decide that the life of a

certain category of people lacks value in and of itself,

other people kill them with impunity and as a matter of course.

—Octavio Paz

A butcher shop on market day in bustling Solola, Guatemala.
Following pages: An altitude camp set up during the ascent of Mount Saint Valentine, 13,300 feet (4,058 m) above sea level in Patagonia, Chile.

October 15

There's a flaw, a secret fissure in the modern intellectual's awareness.

Ripped out of the whole, and the ancient religious absolutes,

we feel a nostalgia for totalities and absolutes.

—Octavio Paz

Resignation is one of our most popular virtues.

We admire fortitude in the face of adversity more than the most brilliant triumph.

—Octavio Paz

These terrestrial turtles found exclusively in the Galápagos Islands of Ecuador are the largest of the species.

You can pick all the flowers but you can't stop the spring.

—Pablo Neruda

Twilight in Salvador da Bahia, Brazil.

Silence is a discussion continued by other means.

—Che Guevara

An old woman in rural Sucre, Bolivia.

Rise and demand, you are flame of fire,

Your conquest is assured where the final horizon

Becomes a drop of blood, a drop of life,

Where your shoulders support the universe,

And on the universe, your hope.

—Miguel Ángel Asturias

A performance by the Ballet Folklórico of Mexico at the Palace of Fine Arts in Mexico City.

Lessen your fear,

because if you let it grow,

it is you who will become small.

—*Amazonian oral tradition*

A young Sarayaku hunter in the Amazon rain forest of Ecuador.

Stoicism is the most exalted of our military and political attributes.

—Octavio Paz

Monumental image of Olmec civilization in La Venta Park in Villahermosa, Mexico.

Following pages: In the heart of Guatemala's Petén rain forest, the ruins of Tikal, the vast religious metropolis of the Mayan world, constitute a major archaeological site.

You must remember the past, not to open old wounds, but to close them.

—Federico Mayor

History is universal, thanks, among other things, to commercial exchange.

At times it has been brother to war;

at others, transmitter of peaceful ideas and beneficial inventions.

I am not suggesting its elimination:

I think that if it is an instrument, it could be transformed into serving justice.

—Octavio Paz

A hardware shop in the market of San Francisco el Alto, Guatemala.

To modernize is to adopt and to adapt, but it is also to re-create.

—Octavio Paz

A bicycle taxi waits for a customer in Havana, Cuba.

Without fraternity, democracy gets waylaid in the nihilism of relativity,

waiting-room for modern societies, trap of nothingness.

—Octavio Paz

With a wingspan of six and a half feet (2 m), the Andean condor lives in the Altiplano mountains at elevations of up to 15,000 feet (4,600 m). This condor is in a zoo in La Paz, Bolivia.

Modernity is both indulgent and rigorous:

it tolerates all sorts of ideas, of temperaments, even of vices,

but it demands—precisely—tolerance.

It is the opposite of fraternity.

—Octavio Paz

A little girl waits while her parents work at repairing a road on the Altiplano in Bolivia.

The most dangerous masses of humanity are the ones whose veins

have been injected with the venom of fear—the fear of change.

—Octavio Paz

A Danzanti mask of the La Paz region on display at the National Museum of Ethnography and Folklore in Sucre, Bolivia.

The lost word must be unearthed,

and we must dream inward and outward…

and there, toward the living center of origin,

beyond end and beginning.

—Octavio Paz

A group of the Raqchi community on the Altiplano of Peru.
Following pages: An isolated village in the Cordillera Apolobamba, Bolivia.

October 29

What democracy cruelly lacks is the other, the others.

—Octavio Paz

Flowers, darling?

Dear little mistress? Won't you buy some squash from me?

They're so good and so cheap.... I'll let you have two for five, my queen.

And you can pick them out yourself, beautiful!

—Luis Cardoza y Aragón

A colorful market scene in San Francisco el Alto, Guatemala.

If the sun is in your heart,

if it gilds your feet and your head,

neither men, gods, nor the elements

can defeat you.

—Miguel Ángel Asturias

In Salvador da Bahia's old city, Brazil.

They will have pity on us, somebody thought, so it wouldn't be strange if they were praying for us.

—Luis Cardoza y Aragón

A village woman prays at the entrance to the church in Angahuan, Mexico.

Traveling teaches us to commit,

to take on the problems of others as if they were our own,

because they are our own.

—Luis Sepúlveda

The bus terminal in San Francisco el Alto, Guatemala.

In some obscure way we realize that life and death are but two phases—

antagonistic but complementary—of a single reality.

Creation and destruction become one in the act of love,

and during a fraction of a second man has a glimpse of a more perfect state of being.

—Octavio Paz

A performance by the Ballet Folklórico of Mexico at the Palace of Fine Arts in Mexico City.

There are invisible passageways between doubt and faith,

freedom is to say "forever" when we say "now,"

it is an oath and it is the art of the transparent enigma:

it is the smile.

—Octavio Paz

The game of seduction on a beach in Salvador da Bahia, Brazil.
Following pages: In the heights of Huehuetenango, Guatemala.

November 5

Everyone is right. And from these rights will be born other new arguments.

—Pablo Neruda

The sun does not set on the horizon.

The sun knows no night,

It's the eye that gets dark, says the painter.

—Fabricio Estrada

A frigate bird soars above the Galápagos, Ecuador.

At your side

light is unnecessary

and honey superfluous.

—Humberto Ak'Abal

Ana Lucia Mendes Dias, seven years old, in Antigua, Guatemala.

Freedom is the choice of necessity.

Let us be the bow and the arrow, the rope and the howl.

The dream is explosive. Brilliant. It returns to the sun.

—Octavio Paz

A festive crowd celebrates carnival in Salvador da Bahia, Brazil.

Better to lose a few battles in the struggle than to lose our dreams without putting up a fight.

—Latin American oral tradition

Farmers returning from the fields in the fertile valley of Fuentes Georginas, Guatemala.

Throw

the

ball

high

EVEN HIGHER

crystal above the universe.

—Orides Fontela

The moon rises on the Bolivian Altiplano, 13,100 feet (4,000 m) above sea level.

One must be humble in order to learn.

—*Maya Quitché oral tradition*

Abuelita, or grandmother, in Potosí, Bolivia.
Following pages: A view of Bolivia's Salar de Uyuni.

November 12

Never surrender your dreams.

It is when we dare not live them

that dreams become impossible.

—Amazonian oral tradition

Could you get into a heated argument (losing peace of mind)

with another person, or with your family,

if it means nothing more to you than proving you are right?

—Martín Aparicio Barrenechea

Socializing at the market in Chivay in the Colca Valley of Peru.

Being right doesn't mean much, no matter how many believe they are.

Right means opinion, and opinion is a partial and insufficient point of view.

One must reach an interior vision of each thing.

One must be an interior vision.

—Roberto Juarroz

Virgin Amazon rain forest in Ecuador.

I keep quiet

to listen to you....

But do not speak

to shut me up.

—Humberto Ak'Abal

Faustina Castillo Alarcon from the village of Chivay in the Colca Valley, Peru.

For a country to fortify and develop its culture, it must open its doors and windows wide

to intellectual, scientific, and artistic currents. It must stimulate the free circulation of ideas—

from wherever they may come—so that local tradition and experience are constantly put to the test;

and so that they may be corrected, completed, and enriched by the traditions and experiences

of those who share the miseries and wonders of the human adventure in other places,

through different languages and circumstances.

—Mario Vargas Llosa

In the old city of Havana, Cuba.

Rights are taken, not asked for; they are seized, not begged for.

—José Martí

A young Amazonian from Brazil.

To escape the vicious circle,

one recommends the gratuitous act.

—Nicanor Parra

A Purépecha village woman on Janitzio Island, Mexico, takes offerings to the cemetery to honor her deceased child.
Following pages: At the market in Zunil, Guatemala.

The oldest sound in the world, the sound of the human heart,

is the matter from which these unforgettable words are formed.

—Pablo Neruda

Perhaps true imagination—as opposed to fantasy—

consists in seeing everyday reality with the eyes of a newborn.

—Octavio Paz

The Jesuit mission in the village of San Miguel de Velasco, Bolivia.

Life is not a trial run, though we try a lot of things;

it is not a fairy tale, though we invent a lot of things;

it is not a poem, though we dream a lot of things.

The test of a tale of the poem of life is its perpetual motion;

this is that perpetual motion.

—Augusto Monterroso

The daughter of a miner in the Cerro Rico mines of Potosí, Bolivia.

If we could but understand a single flower

we might know who we are and what the world is.

—Jorge Luis Borges

The Mayan archaeological site of Tikal emerges from the Petén rain forest in Guatemala.

Be realistic, demand the impossible.

—Che Guevara

An effigy of the revolutionary Ernesto Rafael Guevara de la Serna, better known as Che, in Havana, Cuba.

Utopia is not nowhere:

it is a society, and its inhabitants live communally and scorn gold.

—Carlos Fuentes

At the Sunday market in Tarabuco, Bolivia.

Tupac Amaru, vanquished sun,

a vanished light rises

from your sundered glory

like the sun over the sea.

The deep tribes of clay,

the sacrificed looms,

the wet sand houses

say in silence: "Tupac,"

and Tupac is preserved in the furrow,

they say in silence: "Tupac,"

and Tupac germinates in the ground.

—Pablo Neruda

At the foot of the Villarrica volcano in Atacama, Chile.
Following pages: A fruit vendor in the old city of Cartagena, Colombia.

Thanks be to life that gave me so much.

And your song that is the same song,

And the song of us all, that is still my song.

Thanks be to life that gave me so much.

—Violeta Parra

Beyond being there is still reality, just as beyond the world there is still the cosmos.

—Gladys Olivera Grotti

Descent at twilight from the summit of Chile's Mount Saint Valentine, looking out on Patagonian glaciers, 15,300 feet (4,058 m) above sea level.

Imagine a lamp and make it light.

—Roberto Juarroz

Interior of the Basilica of the Virgin of Guadalupe in Morelia, Mexico.

If a man traveled through Paradise in a dream,

and received a flower as proof of his passage,

then woke to find this flower in his hands… what then?

—Jorge Luis Borges

Wrapped in a shawl and tied to her mother's back, this Bolivian baby seems very content.

It is on the horizon.

I approach two steps, it retreats two steps.

I walk ten steps and the horizon moves ten steps away.

No matter how much I walk, I can never catch up to it.

What's the good of utopia?

It's good for that: for walking.

—Eduardo Galeano

Ascending Mount Anna, 18,000 feet (5,500 m) above sea level, in the Cordillera Apolobamba of Bolivia.

Keep your lamps burning, America

The Incas left more than a small crown of fire and martyrdom in the

amazed hands of history; they left a vast, expansive ambience chiseled by the most

delicate fingers, by hands that could coax melancholy and reverence from sound,

and raise colossal stones to last throughout infinity.

—Pablo Neruda

A stone figure of a Toltec warrior at the National Museum of Anthropology in Mexico City.

A *slow death comes for those who don't revolt when they're unhappy in their work or in love.*

Who don't risk the certain for the uncertain in order to follow a dream.

Who don't allow themselves, at least once in their life, to disregard sensible advice.

—Pablo Neruda

An abandoned pontoon on the San Rafael Lagoon among the fjords of Patagonia, Chile.
Following pages: At the Salar de Uyuni, at 12,000 feet (3,653 m) above sea level, during the rainy season.

December 3

To rise to the sun on the luminous ladder of a sunbeam.

—Rubén Dario

We should sleep with our eyes open, we should dream with our hands.

Let's dream lively dreams of a river probing its banks,

dreams of the sun dreaming its worlds.

Let's dream aloud, let's sing until the song sprouts roots, trunk, branches, birds, stars,

sing until the dream takes root

and the red sprig of resurrection bursts out from the sleeper's side.

—Octavio Paz

A view of Lake Atitlán, Guatemala, in the early morning.

Perhaps reality and unreality do not exist.

Perhaps it is only a question of different levels of reality, some of which we do not perceive.

Or of different levels of unreality, of which we perceive only a few.

Or of different levels of some unique thing, which sometimes we see and sometimes we don't.

—Roberto Juarroz

The road from La Paz, Bolivia, to the Yungas and the Amazon is considered one of the most dangerous roads in the world.

Every person thirsts for wholeness, hungers for communion.

That is why we seek the meaning of our existence,

the link that binds us to the world,

and leads us to take part in time and in its process.

—Octavio Paz

A folkloric troupe dances in front of the church in the village of Yanque, Peru.

We all live in our own world.

But if we observed the starry sky,

we would see that our worlds are different,

that they combine, forging constellations, solar systems, and galaxies.

—Paulo Coelho

In Morelia, Mexico, Maria leaves the Basilica of the Virgin of Guadalupe, where she prays every day.

Understand that none of us is pure,

that we are both real and ideal, heroic and absurd,

made of desire and imagination as much as of blood and bone,

and that each of us is part Christian, part Jew, part Moor,

part Caucasian, part Black, part Indian,

without having to sacrifice any of our components.

—Carlos Fuentes

The capital city of La Paz, Bolivia, 12,100 feet (3,700 m) above sea level.

Nothing has been discovered, because nothing has been totally discovered.

These are nothing but approaches, fragmentary revelations.

Rather than discoveries, we should speak of explorations, of ideas, even of inventions.

—Roberto Juarroz

The guardian of a tobacco-drying barn in Cuba.
Following pages: Crossing the Lusini pass, 16,000 feet (4,900 m) above sea level in the Cordillera Apolobamba of Bolivia.

December 10

We are all Columbuses betting on the reality of our imagination and winning;

we are all Quixotes believing what we imagine.

—Carlos Fuentes

Flying fish, between sky and sea, at once blind and sighted, explode to discover another universe.

How would you like them not to be mute, these flying fish?

What would be their song?

—Luis Cardoza y Aragón

A beach in Cayo Santa Maria, Cuba.

Do we also require a vocation as birds?

A white urgency of seagulls

would launch us, at last,

into the infinite air

to sail interminably

between the blue of the sea and blue of the sky.

—María Teresa Perdomo

Delia, an Aymara girl from Anapia Island on Lake Titicaca in Peru.

The sun will return to your throat,

your forehead, your breast,

before the night of night falls

on your race, on your villages;

and how human will be the cry,

the leap, the dream, the love, and the food.

—Miguel Ángel Asturias

In the mountains of Sucre, Bolivia.

I *only*

think

that I've perhaps been worthy of so much

simplicity, of a flower so pure,

that perhaps I'm you, that's right,

that bit of earth, flour, and song,

that natural batch that knows

whence it comes and where it belongs.

—Pablo Neruda

The busy Sunday market in Tarabuco, Bolivia, 10,500 feet (3,200 m) above sea level.

Greetings, and let the dance begin!

Our songs rose higher than our mountains, and they will be heard here;

our dances were more persistent than the ocean waves, and will be presented here.

Let us defend this delicate strength, let us defend the unity of love and peace

that kept them alive. This is the duty of all men, the central

treasure of peoples, the light of this festival.

—Pablo Neruda

A dance lesson in Antigua, Guatemala.

Order becomes beauty

beyond infinite planes

and the undeciphered dense text

a mosaic flower, fiery.

Chaos tamed in fullness,

spring.

—Orides Fontela

The courtyard of the cathedral in Morelia, Mexico, in November.
Following pages: A happy encounter in Antigua, Guatemala.

The words looked forward to kissing you.

The word. That's what hope could be: a word.

—Miguel Ángel Asturias

And so for a thousand years

you wait for the return of your cities:

the one with the green and fragrant soil,

the one where the day was colored by the sun blind with gold,

the one with the new amaranths hanging from the stars,

the one with the clawed silbo with soft pointed feathers,

the one with the heat wave and simple sea of pearls,

the one that governs the fat raindrops,

and the one with your hope, volcano of the green day.

—Miguel Ángel Asturias

Named for the Quechua word for "old mountain," Machu Picchu—7,800 feet (2,400 m)—
is the most important Inca archaeological site in Peru.

Today it is you, and tomorrow

another like you will carry on and wait.

There is no hurry, no demands.

Humankind will not come to an end.

Here was a valley, now there arises a mountain.

Where there was a hill, now there's a ravine.

The petrified sea turned into a mountain

and lightning crystallized into lakes.

—Miguel Ángel Asturias

A villager from the Tarabuco region during the annual Phujllay festival.

All is possible.

Nothing should be disdained.

Nothing is incredible.

Nothing is impossible.

The possibilities that we deny are but the possibilities that we ignore.

—Carlos Fuentes

A representation of Death from Teotihuacán at the National Museum of Anthropology in Mexico City.

There is a time of evening when the prairie is about to say something.

It *never says it.*

Or perhaps it is constantly saying it but we never hear it,

or we hear it, but it is as inexpressible as a piece of music.

—Jorge Luis Borges

The sun sets on the Coipasa salt flat in Bolivia.

What is the song of the birds, Adam?

For the birds themselves become air.

To sing is to spill over into drops of air, into strands of air, to vibrate.

—Jaime Sabines

A seagull flies over the San Rafael Lagoon in Patagonia, Chile.

Talking with the things and with ourselves

the universe talks to itself:

we are its tongue and ears,

its words and silences.

—Octavio Paz

Voladores, the "birdmen," performing the flying dance, a very ancient ritual of the Totonac people of Mexico.
Following pages: A sea lion on North Seymour Island in the Galápagos, Ecuador.

December 24

There is no end; everything has been a perpetual beginning all over again.

—Octavio Paz

I am proud that I belong to all humanity,

not to a few but to many,

and that here I am surrounded by their invisible presence.

—Pablo Neruda

In the tail of a Caribbean cyclone.

Every moon, every year, every day, every wind comes along and then departs.

In the same way, our blood courses toward its resting place.

—CHILAM BALAM, *ancient Mayan text*

Ascending Mount Anna, 18,000 feet (5,500 m) above sea level in the Cordillera Apolobamba, Bolivia.

There is no proposition that does not imply the entire universe;

to say "the jaguar" is to say all the jaguars that engendered it,

the deer and turtles it has devoured,

the grass that fed the deer,

the earth that was mother to the grass,

the sky that gave light to the earth.

—Jorge Luis Borges

A Charapa turtle at the Fatima de Puyo Center for endangered species in the Amazon region of Ecuador.

Title of my days, adorable,

and in space you occupy, like the day,

all the light that the universe possesses.

—Pablo Neruda

Misha Malaver, three years old, a child in Sarayaku, Amazonian Ecuador.

You brim the curvature of silence.

—Pablo Neruda

Ascending the cone of ashes at the summit of the highly active Pacaya volcano, 8,500 feet (2,600 m) above sea level in Guatemala.

When you close your eyes, I will go to sleep.

—Pablo Neruda

Guatemalan fabrics are among the most colorful in Latin America.
Following pages: Cécilia Antequera Camacho and Ulio Santander on Salar de Uyuni, the vast salt flat in Bolivia.

December 31

I want

to do with you what spring does with the cherry trees.

—Pablo Neruda

BIOGRAPHIES

Danielle Pons-Föllmi was born and raised in Latin America. She discovered Europe at the age of seventeen. With her background at the crossroads of civilizations, Föllmi developed an early taste for the mixing of cultures. She studied tropical medicine in Paris and served as a physician on missions to Panama, India, Cambodia, and Laos. In Switzerland, she specialized in anesthesiology and intensive care. She married Olivier Föllmi, with whom she shares an intellectual synergy—combining passion and destiny through twenty years of traveling—that has led to the publication of twenty-three books as well as the founding of HOPE, a nonprofit organization dedicated to furthering education and village mutual aid for the benefit of those who humbly contribute to the "wisdom of humanity" throughout the world (www.hope-organisation.com). This lifelong journey, based upon experience and multicultural, multidisciplinary perspectives, has inspired Danielle Föllmi to expand her knowledge of human nature: in her probing research, she seeks to connect the body, the heart, and the mind. She and her husband have developed the comprehensive Offerings for Humanity book series that captures and seeks to perpetuate the knowledge and wisdom of the great cultural traditions that constitute humanity's heritage.

Photographer **Olivier Föllmi** spent seven months traveling through Latin America—from Patagonia to the coasts of the Caribbean, from the Galápagos Islands to the Amazon rain forest—to gather the 365 images featured in this book. Born in 1958, Olivier Föllmi grew up in the French and Swiss Alps. In 2003, after living with the Tibetan people in the Himalayas for twenty years, he and his wife began traveling the world on behalf of the Offerings for Humanity project. Föllmi uses photography to extol men and women whose humaneness contributes to a future filled with the possibility for cultural reciprocity and tolerance. This book, his twenty-third, is translated into seven languages and published in ten countries.

Humberto Ak'Abal is a Maya Quitché poet born in Guatemala in 1952. He left school at twelve and worked at a variety of odd jobs before devoting himself to poetry. Ak'Abal writes in his native tongue, Quitché, before translating his work into Spanish himself. A collection of his work, *Poems I Brought Down from the Mountain*, was published in 1999.

A major Latin American writer, **Claribel Alegría** was born in 1924 in Estelí, Nicaragua, to Salvadoran parents. After receiving a degree in philosophy and literature from George Washington University in the United States, she lived abroad for many years. A member of the politically engaged "committed generation," she took part in the Central American literary revival of the 1960s; her revolutionary poetry focuses on a denunciation of social injustices. Associated with the Sandinistas, the movement that overthrew the dictator Somoza in 1979, she returned to Nicaragua in 1985; an edition of *Death of Somoza*, a nonfiction work, appeared in 1996. Claribel Alegría has published over forty books, including poetry, novels, short stories for children, and nonfiction. Her many volumes of acclaimed poetry include *Thresholds/Umbrales*, 1996, and *Saudade* (Sorrow), 1999, which expresses her grief at the death of her husband, Darwin Flakoll, who was also her translator and collaborator. In 1978,

Alegría was awarded the prestigious prize of the Casas de las Américas in Havana for her poetry collection *Sobrevivo* (I Survive), published in 1978.

Mexican novelist **Homero Aridjis** was born in 1940 in Contepec, in the state of Michoacán. He has published many novels, including *1492: The Life and Times of Juan Cabezón of Castile*, 1992, a tribute to Mexican civilization. The founder of the journal *Correspondancias*, he is also president of the Group of One Hundred, an environmental movement of artists, intellectuals, and scientists.

Miguel Ángel Asturias (1899–1974), the acclaimed Guatemalan writer, was born in Guatemala City in 1899, of Maya origin on his mother's side. He attended university in his native city and later studied at the Sorbonne. For his fiction and poetry, which tirelessly condemn imperialism, Asturias was awarded the 1966 Lenin Peace Prize and the 1967 Nobel Prize in Literature. His major works include *Legends of Guatemala*, 1930; *Mulata*, 1963; and *Men of Maize*, 1995. The Nobel Prize Committee commended Asturias for his "vivid literary achievement, deep-rooted in the national traits and traditions of Indian peoples of Latin America."

Patricio Atkinson is a human rights activist and teacher in Guatemala. In 1991 he founded the *Asociación Nuestros Ahijados*, Our Godchild Association, which is active in many Third World countries.

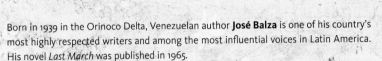

Born in 1939 in the Orinoco Delta, Venezuelan author **José Balza** is one of his country's most highly respected writers and among the most influential voices in Latin America. His novel *Last March* was published in 1965.

Apolonio Bartolo Ronquillo was born in 1961 in a Mazatec community in San Miguel Soyaltepec, Oaxaca, Mexico. A bilingual teacher and cultural administrator, he holds a degree in Indian Education. His work as a Mazatec poet appears in regional as well as national magazines and newspapers, including the bilingual publication *Alas del viento/Tjiunga'e Tjao*, 1998. Ronquillo is a founding member of the Organization for Research in Mazatec Culture (OIMAC) and the Association of Writers in Indigenous Languages. Currently he is coordinator of research and professional training at the Center for Writers in Indigenous Languages in Mexico City.

Mario Benedetti was born in Uruguay in 1920. A prolific and versatile writer, he is an important figure of Latin American literature. He studied at the German high school in Montevideo, Uruguay, an experience that inspired his early writings. The triumph of the Cuban revolution in 1960, the year that he published his brief, touching love story, *The Truce*, proved a turning point for Benedetti. His subsequent commitment to political activism is echoed in his diverse writings, which include novels, short stories, essays, and songs, along with many works of poetry, beginning with his first collection, *La vispera indeleble*, 1985, through a recent bilingual edition, *Little Stones at My Window*, 2003. In 1968, he created Las Casas de las Américas in Havana as a center for literary research.

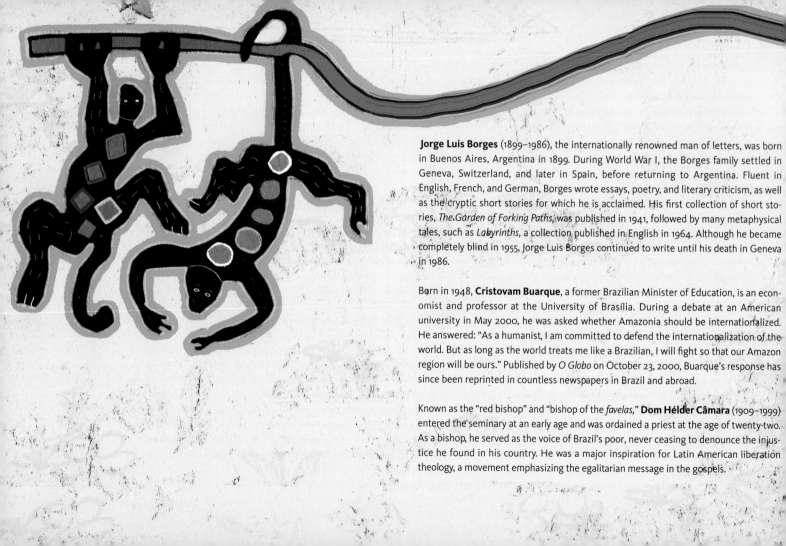

Jorge Luis Borges (1899–1986), the internationally renowned man of letters, was born in Buenos Aires, Argentina in 1899. During World War I, the Borges family settled in Geneva, Switzerland, and later in Spain, before returning to Argentina. Fluent in English, French, and German, Borges wrote essays, poetry, and literary criticism, as well as the cryptic short stories for which he is acclaimed. His first collection of short stories, *The Garden of Forking Paths*, was published in 1941, followed by many metaphysical tales, such as *Labyrinths*, a collection published in English in 1964. Although he became completely blind in 1955, Jorge Luis Borges continued to write until his death in Geneva in 1986.

Born in 1948, **Cristovam Buarque**, a former Brazilian Minister of Education, is an economist and professor at the University of Brasília. During a debate at an American university in May 2000, he was asked whether Amazonia should be internationalized. He answered: "As a humanist, I am committed to defend the internationalization of the world. But as long as the world treats me like a Brazilian, I will fight so that our Amazon region will be ours." Published by *O Globo* on October 23, 2000, Buarque's response has since been reprinted in countless newspapers in Brazil and abroad.

Known as the "red bishop" and "bishop of the *favelas*," **Dom Hélder Câmara** (1909–1999) entered the seminary at an early age and was ordained a priest at the age of twenty-two. As a bishop, he served as the voice of Brazil's poor, never ceasing to denounce the injustice he found in his country. He was a major inspiration for Latin American liberation theology, a movement emphasizing the egalitarian message in the gospels.

Guatemalan writer **Luis Cardoza y Aragón** (1901–1992) spent his youth in Paris where he witnessed the birth of surrealism. He combined aesthetics and politics with a baroque Latin American and tropical sensibility reminiscent of the art of Mexican murals. His collection of essays, *Guatemala: las líneas de su mano* (Guatemala: The Lines of Its Hand), 1995, remains an important manifesto for Latin American intellectuals. He spent many years in exile and died in Mexico.

The Guatemalan poet and intellectual **Ismaël Cerna** (1856–1901) earned a degree in philosophy and then studied medicine and law but never practiced. At the fall of the government of his uncle, Vicente Cerna, he was arrested, and lived much of his life in exile and in prison. His most beautiful poems were written in a prison cell.

Paulo Coelho was born in Rio de Janeiro, Brazil, in 1947. Before gaining fame for his international best-sellers, he was a playwright and journalist, as well as a songwriter for some of the most popular stars of Brazilian music, among them Elis Règina and Raul Seixas. Coelho has an authentic gift for evoking the individual, the world, and the ties that bind them, for which he enjoys an intimacy with his readers. His most famous work, *The Alchemist,* which first appeared in Brazil in 1988, was published in 150 countries and sold more than 30 million copies worldwide. Coelho is a member of the Brazilian Academy of Letters.

Writer **Francisco Coloane** (1910–2002) was born in 1910 on Chiloe Island in southern Chile. One of the great Chilean writers of the twentieth century, Coloane chronicled the lives of peasants, hunters, and, particularly, sailors in southern Chile. A new edition of *Cape Horn and Other Stories from the End of the World* was published in 2003.

Rubén Darío (1867–1916), was born in Nicaragua. A constant wanderer and a great defender of Latin American identity, he began his literary career with a series of articles opposing the Nicaraguan government. An admirer of the Parnassans—he met Verlaine in Paris—this modernist master wrote many collections of poetry, among them the highly influential *Azul* (Blue), published in 1888, and *Songs of Life and Hope,* 2004. He died in poverty in Nicaragua in 1916.

Born in La Paz, Bolivia in 1934, **Enrique Dussel** is a professor of ethics, a philosopher, and a theologian. An Argentine living and teaching in Mexico, Dussel is one of the most original and creative Latin American critical thinkers. *The Invention of the Americas: Eclipse of "the Other" and the Myth of Modernity* was published in 1995.

Born in 1974, **Fabricio Estrada** is recognized in Honduras for his optimistic poetic works. His most recent publication is a collection of poems, *Solares,* 2004.

After studying philosophy, **Orides Fontela** (1949–1998) worked as a school librarian in the poor suburbs of Sao Paulo, Brazil, for many years. She died of tuberculosis in poverty and obscurity. Along with five volumes of poetry, among them *Alba* (Dawn), published in 1983, Fontela also wrote a play. Her poems lucidly reconcile the aristocratic demands of meditation and the strict simplicity of her origins.

Carlos Fuentes was born in Panama City in 1928, the son of a Mexican diplomat. He received a law degree from the National University of Mexico, but pursued a career as a journalist and writer. He became an emblematic figure of Latin American literature through his experiments with the novel, as well as the short story, drama, and the literary and political essay. His work explores Latin American culture and Mexican history as well as modernist themes of time and identity. Widely published in Latin America, the United States, and Europe, Fuentes was awarded the Cervantes Prize. His acclaimed novels include *The Death of Artemio Cruz*, 1965; *Terra Nostra*, 1975; and *The Old Gringo*, 1985, which was made into an American film.

Eduardo Galeano was born in 1940 in Montevideo, Uruguay. At the age of fourteen, he traveled extensively through Latin America and began a career as a journalist. He served as editor in chief of the weekly *Marcha*, and then as managing director of the newspaper *Epoca*. *The Open Veins of Latin America*, a cultural and political critique, was published in 1971. Forced into exile in Argentina and, later, in Spain, Galeano returned to Uruguay in 1985. *The Book of Embraces*, a literary work, was published in 1989.

Salvadoran poet, novelist, and storyteller **David Escobar Galindo** was born in 1943. He holds a doctorate in law and social science. His poetry collections include *Libro de Lillian* (Lillian's Book), 1976, and, most recently, *Libro del fiel* (The Needle Book), 2004.

Gabriel García Márquez, the internationally renowned Colombian novelist, journalist, and political activist, was born in Aracataca, a village in northern Colombia, in 1928. He is identified with the literary style of magical realism. He began his career as a journalist in Colombia, later serving as a correspondent in Paris, Rome, Barcelona, Caracas, and New York. At the same time, he pursued his literary activities: his masterpiece is *One Hundred Years of Solitude*, 1967, a novel that explores the lives of several generations of a family living in a fictional city; another important novel, *Love in the Time of Cholera*, was published in 1985. In 1982, Gabriel Garcia Márquez was awarded the Nobel Prize in Literature.

Guatemalan poet **Otto Raúl González** was born in 1921. Under the dictatorship of Jorge Ubico, he was exiled in 1944 and has been living in Mexico since 1954. The poetry that he wrote between 1943 and 1967 is collected in *Poesía fundamental*, 1973. In 1990, he received the Jaime Sabines Award.

Ernesto Guevara de la Serna (1928–1967), better known as **Che**, was an iconic communist revolutionary and political figure, born and raised in Argentina. A close collaborator of Fidel Castro during the Cuban revolution, Che became one of the principal leaders of the new Cuban state. In 1967, he left for Bolivia, where he was captured and executed by the Bolivian army. Che Guevara's early diaries were published in English as *The Motorcycle Diaries: Notes on a Latin American Journey*, and were made into a noteworthy film in 2004.

Born into a working-class background in Cuba in 1904, **Nicolas Guillén** is the leading Cuban poet of the twentieth century. Guillén practiced law before turning to journalism and founding the magazine *Lirio* in 1923. He published his first poems, *Motivos de son* (The Reasons for Sound), 1930, in a Havana literary journal. Inspired by the Afro-Cuban musical tradition, poetry collections such as *Yoruba from Cuba*, 2004, draw their themes from the life and language of blacks and mulattos in Havana. Praising the mixing of black and European cultures and calling for respect for every human being, Guillén's work reflects his rejection of injustice, colonization, and imperialism.

Thilda Herbillon-Moubayed was born in Beirut, Lebanon, in 1951. Holding a doctorate in Education, Herbillon-Moubayed taught at the Catholic Institute of Paris XII and at the University René Descartes-Paris V before joining the *Groupe d'Enseignement de L'Espace Urbain*, Group for Teaching the Management of Urban Space, in Lyon and Paris. *La danse, conscience du vivant: étude anthropologique et esthétique* (Dance, Consciousness of Life: An Anthropological and Aesthetic Study), was published by the *Groupe d'Enseignement* in 2005.

Born in 1806, **Benito Juárez** (1806–1872) was the first indigenous president of Mexico. He lived in his native village until the age of twelve and dedicated his life to native communities. At first a lawyer, Juárez was governor of the state of Oaxaca from 1847 to 1852. He went into exile in the United States during the reign of Emperor Maximilian, took part in the Revolution of Ayutla, and was eventually elected president of Mexico. Juárez twice served as president—from 1861 to 1863, and from 1867 until his death in 1872. Nearly every Mexican town has a street named after this hero of progressive reform.

Born in Argentina in 1925, **Roberto Juarroz** studied literature and philosophy at the University of Buenos Aires. Editor of the magazine *Poesia* from 1958 to 1965 and translator of poets such as Antonin Artaud, he also contributed to many journals as a literary and film critic. His poetry collections, first published in 1976, have a single title, *Vertical Poetry*, with each volume numbered to distinguish it from the others.

Hugo Lindo (1917–1985), a Salvadoran lawyer, diplomat, literary critic, and poet, has had a great influence on the literature of El Salvador. A collection of his poetry, *The Ways of Rain*, was published in 1986.

J. M. (Joaquim Mario) Machado de Assis (1839–1908) was born in Rio de Janeiro, Brazil, in 1839. After working at various professions, including printing, he began to contribute to numerous literary journals and magazines. Poet, novelist, and storyteller, he was one of the major Brazilian writers of the nineteenth century. His novels include *Philosopher or Dog?*, originally published in 1891, and *Dom Casmurro*, 1899. Machado de Assis founded the Brazilian Academy of Letters in 1867.

José Martí (1853–1895) is undoubtedly the figure most adored by the Cuban people, who consider him their greatest martyr and the apostle of the fight for independence. Born in Havana in 1853, the son of a Spanish immigrant, Martí became involved in the anti-colonial struggle at an early age. At fifteen, he founded a nationalist newspaper. At sixteen, he was arrested for treason and sentenced to six years of hard labor. Freed six months later, he was deported to Spain, where he remained for four years. His years of exile continued in France, England, Mexico, and New York, where he dedicated himself to obtaining Cuban independence in his work with the Cuban revolutionary party. At the head of a military expedition intended to liberate Cuba in 1895, he was killed during his first battle. Martí was also a poet and writer: some of his work is collected in the *José Martí Reader: Writings on the Americas*, 1999, and *José Martí: Major Poems*, 1982.

Federico Mayor was born in Barcelona in 1934. Educated in biochemistry, which he teaches in Granada and Madrid, Mayor served as director general of UNESCO, the United Nations Educational, Scientific, and Cultural Organization, from 1987 to 1999. He is the author of scientific publications; four collections of poetry; and a collection of essays, *The World Ahead: Our Future in the Making*, published in 1999.

Rigoberta Menchú is a Maya Quitché activist born in 1959 in Guatemala. Her father fought for native land and civil rights, and her entire family was massacred by military troops. Her own struggle for the indigenous people of Guatemala is reflected in her book *I, Rigoberta Menchú*, written with Elisabeth Burgos-Debray and published in 1983. She was awarded the Nobel Peace Prize in 1992.

On November 15, 1945, the first Nobel Prize in Literature awarded to a Latin American writer was presented to **Gabriela Mistral** (1889–1957). Born in the small Chilean village of Vicuña, Mistral worked as a rural schoolteacher throughout her native country. She then participated in the reform of the education system in Mexico. Her first revelatory collection of poetry, *Los sonetos de la muerte* (Sonnets of Death), written following the suicide of her fiancé, appeared in *Desolation,* a collection published in 1922. Mistral pursued her poetry at the same time that she served as a diplomat in Naples, Madrid, and Lisbon. Never forgetting her beginnings, the former schoolteacher devoted some of her most beautiful poems to children.

One of the most important Guatemalan writers, **Augusto Monterroso** (1921–2003) was born in Honduras. His work is multilayered, eccentric, and playful, characterized by diverse reflections, tales, fragments, and quotations assembled into odd collages. In works such as "Perpetual Motion," collected in *The Complete Works and Other Stories,* 1996, Monterroso questions life through riddles. He claimed to have written the shortest novel in literature: "When he awakened, the dinosaur was always there." Monterroso is a unique figure in Latin American literature.

Born in Guatemala, **Roberto Monzón** (1948–1992) studied history before joining the guerilla movement. For many years, he personally published and sold his books.

Vinícius de Moraes (1913–1980) is one of the key figures of contemporary Brazilian music. The lyricist of many classics of Brazilian popular music, he was the co-writer of nearly 400 songs. Vinícius de Moraes is known for his duets with Maria Creuza, Toquinho, and Tom Jobim.

Edmond Mulet, born in 1951, was elected several times to the Chamber of Deputies in his native Guatemala. He has served as president of the National Assembly and as ambassador to the United States and various European countries. He has also worked as a journalist. An opponent of the former military regimes in Guatemala, Mulet continues to fight for democracy and the rights of indigenous peoples. He has been posted in Haiti since June 2006 as special representative of Secretary General Kofi Annan and head of the United Nations Mission for the Stabilization of Haiti.

The great Chilean poet Neftali Ricardo Reyes, better known as **Pablo Neruda** (1904–1973), was born in modest circumstances. He began to write as a teenager and was soon balancing literary and political careers: his life would be characterized by trips abroad and exile. After holding several diplomatic posts beginning in 1927, Pablo Neruda was elected senator for the mining provinces in the north of Chile. Persecuted as a communist by President Gabriel Gonzales Videla, Neruda was forced to flee his country. In 1970, he was appointed Chilean ambassador to France by socialist president Salvador Allende. In 1971, the politically engaged poet received the Nobel Prize in Literature, cited for his monumental poetic work inspired by political struggle and revolt—*Canto General,* 1950—as well as the delicate lyricism of *Twenty Love Poems and a Song of Despair,* 1924. Neruda is the Chilean poet of love and the earth.

Juan Carlos Onetti (1909–1994) was born in Montevideo, Uruguay. The author of many novels, short stories, essays, and poems, he pursued a literary career while working as a journalist. Works such as *The Pit*, 1939, and *No Man's Land*, 1941, have contributed to Onetti's reputation as a precursor of the French *nouveau roman*, the new novel. In 1980, Onetti won the prestigious Cervantes Prize.

Born in Mexico in 1939, **José Emilio Pacheco** is a major Latin American poet. He is also a novelist, publisher, and prolific translator. *Don't Ask Me How the Time Goes By: Poems, 1964–1968*, published in 1978, and *Tree between Two Walls*, 1996, are two of his poetry collections. An edition of his avant-garde novel, *A Distant Death*, was published in 1977. Pacheco was director of the library collection at the National University of Mexico and holds honorary degrees from many international universities.

Chilean poet **Nicanor Parra** was born in 1914 in southern Chile. His poetry, often called "antipoetry," has been translated into several languages: *Antipoems: How to Look Better and Feel Great* was published in 2004. A significant figure in Chilean literature, he has received numerous national and international awards. He is the brother of Violeta Parra.

Violeta Parra (1917–1967) was born in 1917 in San Carlos, a village in southern Chile. The daughter of a farm woman and a teacher, she was attracted to the traditional songs she heard first from her mother. At twelve, she composed her first songs, accompanying herself on the guitar. Violeta Parra later settled in Santiago de Chile. She got off to a rough start, performing in bars, circuses, and on the radio; she sang popular songs and romantic boleros before dedicating herself to the composition and performance of folk music. Violetta Parra was an inspiration to *La Nueva Canción*, the New Song movement;

"*Gracias a la vida,*" or "Thanks Be to Life," remains one of Latin America's most famous songs. Parra committed suicide in 1967.

The renowned poet, novelist, and cultural critic **Octavio Paz** (1914–1998) was born in Mexico City in 1914. He was one of the first novelists to write about the lives of Mexican Indians. As a young man, Paz traveled in the United States and immersed himself in modern Anglo-American poetry. Like some other Latin American writers, he joined the diplomatic corps and was posted to France, where he wrote his essential study of Mexican identity, *The Labyrinth of Solitude,* 1962. He also played an active role in publications of the Surrealist movement. In 1962, Paz was appointed Mexican ambassador to India. After having received many prestigious prizes, Octavio Paz was awarded in 1990 the greatest distinction of them all, the Nobel Prize in Literature. *The Collected Poems of Octavio Paz, 1957–1987,* was published in 1991. At the time of his death in 1998, Paz was a universally acclaimed literary figure.

María Teresa Perdomo is a contemporary Mexican poet from the state of Michoacán. Her book *Periferias* (Peripheries) was published in 1982 in Mexico.

Comic-strip artist Joaquín Salvador Lavado, known as **Quino,** was born in 1932 in Argentina. He attended art school in Mendoza before settling in Buenos Aires, where his drawings were published in various magazines. Quino is both artist and scriptwriter: after ten years of publishing gritty cartoon humor, he created the character of Mafalda, a girl who observes the world with a critical eye. His book *Mafalda and Friends* appeared in 2004. In 1982, he was declared "comic artist of the year" by an international panel of his colleagues.

Born in El Salvador, postmodern poet **Serafín Quiteño** (1906–1987) brought provincial color and honesty to Salvadoran poetry. His collection of poetry *Corazón con S* (Heart with an S) was published in 1941, and *Tórrido sueño* (Torrid Dreams) in 1957.

Mexican poet **Roberto Reséndiz Carmona** was born in 1954 in Zitácuaro, Michoacán, and settled in Zamora in 1976. His earliest poems appeared in newspapers and magazines in Zamora, Morelia, and Guadalajara. In 1982, his first poetry collection, *Poemas de espejo* (Mirror Poems), was published in Zamora. Other works would follow, among them *La noche rueda del tintero* (The Inkpot's Night Wheel) in 1985, and *De Peces y Colores* (Of Fish and Colors) in 1999.

Augusto Roa Bastos (1917–2005) was born in Asunción, Paraguay. Roa Bastos's eclectic career included turns as screenwriter, playwright, journalist, and as a professor in a number of universities. Having settled in France in 1976, Roa Bastos taught Latin American literature at the University of Toulouse until 1983. He is the author of more than twenty books, including novels—among them *I, The Supreme,* 1974, and *Son of Man,* 1960—short stories, and plays translated into twenty-five languages. He was awarded the prestigious Cervantes Prize in 1989.

Jaime Sabines (1926–1999) was born in Chiapas, Mexico, the son of a Lebanese immigrant. He studied medicine and literature at the National University of Mexico. He has long been one of the most popular Mexican poets, whose work has been collected in *Recuento de poemas, 1950–1993,* published in 1997. *On the Death of Major Sabines* is one of the major works of Hispanic literature.

Luis Sepúlveda was born in 1949 in Orvalle, a small town in the north of Chile. As a student, he was imprisoned and tortured by the Pinochet regime. Following a summary trial by a military tribunal, he was condemned to twenty-eight years in prison. Thanks to the efforts of Amnesty International, he was freed, but he was then exiled to Sweden for eight years. He later lived in Ecuador, Peru, Colombia, and Nicaragua. Concerned about the fate of Amazonian peoples, Sepúlveda spent a year with the Shuar Indians in 1978 as part of a UNESCO research program. He is a regular contributor to the Spanish newspaper *El País* and to various Italian newspapers. Sepúlveda's first novel, *The Old Man Who Read Love Stories*, 1995, was translated into thirty-five languages and gained him world fame.

Born in Montevideo, Uruguay, in 1957, **Magdelena Thompson** is a published poet who also practices medicine.

Mario Vargas Llosa was born in Arequipa, Peru, in 1936. He spent his childhood in Cochabamba, Bolivia, and in Piura, in the north of Peru. At the age of fourteen, he was sent to the Leoncio Prado military academy in Lima, a haunting experience that spawned one of his major novels, *La cuidad y los perros*, 1962, published in English as *The Time of the Hero* in 1963. Vargas Llosa honed his literary skills through journalism before receiving his doctorate in literature in Madrid, where he wrote a dissertation on Gabriel García Márquez. His novels, including *The War of the End of the World*, 1981; *Aunt Julia and the Scriptwriter*, 1982; and *The Feast of the Goat*, translated into English in 2001, encompass a broad social panorama as well as modernist themes and techniques. Today, he is widely recognized for his novels, essays, and literary and cultural criticism, and he regularly lectures at universities throughout the world. In 1990, he was a candidate for president of Peru, but was defeated by Alberto Fujimori.

A writer and philosopher born in Mexico City in 1912, **Leopoldo Zea** is one of the most significant Latin American thinkers of the twentieth century. In 1952, he initiated the Mexico and Mexican Identity book series, publishing numerous seminal works. In addition to his work as a publisher and as a university professor, Zea is the author of many works on Latin American philosophy, thought, and culture, among them *The Latin American Mind*, 1963, and *Latin America and the World*, 1969.

Ak'Abal, Humberto. *Con los ojos después del mar*. Mexico: Editorial Praxis, 2000: Feb 19; Jul 16.

Ak'Abal, Humberto. *Entre patojos*. Guatemala: Piedra Santa, 2005: Feb 7, 11; Jun 5, 7; Aug 27.

Ak'Abal, Humberto. *Kamayoyik*. Guatemala: Cholsamaj, 2002: Sept 26; Nov 7, 15.

Aparicio Barrenechea, Martín. *Conciencia de si*. Mexico: 2002: Nov 13.

Aridjis, Homero. *Los poemas solares*. Mexico: Fondo de Cultura Económica, 2005: Jul 3; Aug 19; Nov 6.

Asturias, Miguel Ángel. *Obras Completas*. Madrid: Aguilar, 1969.

Asturias, Miguel Ángel. *Poèmes indiens*. Translated by Claude Couffon and René-L.-F. Durand. Paris: Gallimard, 1990: Jan 25, 30; Feb 6; Mar 26; Apr 22; May 7; Jun 30; Aug 29; Sept 16; Oct 12, 31; Dec 13, 17–19.

Asturias, Miguel Ángel. *Tres de Cuatro Soles*. Paris: Klincksieck, 1977: Jan 7; Feb 16; Apr 20; May 20; Jul 4; Aug 31.

Balza, José. *La Fleur de minuit*. Translated by Claude Fell. Paris: Gallimard, 1992: May 19.

Bartolo Ronquillo, Apolonio. *Alas del viento*. Mexico: Letras indígenas contemporáneas, 1998: Mar 12; May 10.

Benedetti, Mario. *Antología des poetica*. Madrid: Alianza Editorial, 1997: Aug 16.

Borges, Jorge Luis, and Ernesto Sabato. *Conversations à Buenos Aires*. Edited by Orlando Barone. Translated by Michel Bibard. Paris: 10/18, 2001: Feb 2; Apr 15; Jul 12.

Borges, Jorge Luis. *The Aleph and Other Stories*. Translated by Andrew Hurley. New York: Penguin, 1998: Mar 11; May 29; Jul 1; Sept 17; Nov 22; Dec 27.

Burgos-Debray, Elisabeth. *Moi, Rigoberta Menchù*. Translated by Michèle Goldstein. Paris: Gallimard, 1983: Mar 10; May 22; Oct 19.

Cardoza y Aragón, Luis. *Guatemala, Las líneas de su mano*.

San Carlos, Guatemala: Editorial Universitaria Universidad de San Carlos de Guatemala, 2003: Jan 8, 10, 15, 16, 20, 21, 26, 31; Feb 5, 15, 28; Mar 15; Apr 6; May 23; Jun 2, 10; Sept 15; Oct 30; Nov 1; Dec 11.

Coelho, Paulo. *The Alchemist*. Translated by Alan Clarke. San Francisco, CA: Harper San Francisco, 1993: Mar 7; Apr 16; Jun 28.

Coelho, Pablo. *Palabras esenciales*. Buenos Aires: V1R Editorias (Vergara & Riba), 1998: Feb 20; Dec 7.

Dictionnaire de citations du monde entier. Paris: Dictionnaires Le Robert, 2002: Feb 4; Apr 2; May 25–27; Jun 15; Jul 25; Aug 12; Sept 2, 20, 27; Oct 1; Nov 18; Dec 3, 10; back endpaper.

Estrada, Fabricio. *Solares*. Tegucigalpa, Honduras: Pez Dulce, 2004: Jan 27.

Fontela, Orides. *Rosace*. Translated by Emmanuel Jaffelin and Marcio de Lima Dantas. Paris: L'Harmattan, 1999: Mar 8; Jul 23; Nov 10; Dec 16.

Fontela, Orides. *Trèfles-Trevo*. Paris: L'Harmattan, 1988: Apr 9, 13; May 1; Jun 21; Aug 22; Sept 23.

Fuentes, Carlos. *Buried Mirror*. New York: Houghton Mifflin Company, 1992: Feb 8; Mar 18, 24, 27; May 21; Jun 3; Aug 1; Sept 30; Oct 10; Nov 24; Dec 8, 20.

García Márquez, Gabriel. *In Evil Hour*. Translated by Gregory Rabassa. New York: Harper & Row, 1979: Aug 26.

Galeano, Eduardo. *El libro de los abrazos/Imagenes y palabras*. Madrid: Siglo veintiuno de Espana, 2004: Mar 9.

Galeano, Eduardo. *Las palabras andantes con grabados de José Borges*. España Editores, 2000: Mar 25; Nov 30.

Gonzalez, Otto Raúl. *Poseía Fundamental*. San Carlos, Guatemala: Editorial Universitaria Universidad de San Carlos de Guatemala, 1995: Jan 4, 19; Apr 5.

Herbillon-Moubayed, Thilda. *La danse, conscience du vivant*. Paris: L'Harmattan, 2005: Jul 7, 15.

Juárez, Benito. *Flor y latigo idearío político*. Mexico: Edicion

del Noletin, 1957: Sept 8.

Juarroz, Roberto. *Fragments verticaux*. Translated by Silvia Baron Supervielle. Paris: José Corti, 1994: Mar 13; Apr 19, 24; Aug 2; Nov 14, 28; Dec 5, 9.

Le Goff, Marcel. *Jorge Luis Borges, L'Univers, la lettre et le secret*. Paris: L'Harmattan, 1999: Apr 4, 27; May 14; Jun 1, 24; Jul 21; Aug 3, 18, 24; Nov 29; Dec 21.

Machado de Assis, Joachim Maria. *La Théorie du médaillon*. Translated by Florent Kohler. Paris: Métailié, 2002: Jun 16.

Mellac, Régine, ed. and trans. *Chants libres d'Amérique latine*. Paris: Cerf, 1978: Feb 1, 21; May 3; Jul 9; Aug 8; Nov 26.

Mistral, Gabriela. *Selected Poems*. Translated by Ursula K. Le Guin. Albuquerque, NM: University of New Mexico Press, 2003: Apr 30; May 8; Jun 29; Aug 20.

Monterroso, Augusto. *La oveja negra y demás fábulas*. Mexico: Premio príncipe de Asturias de las letras, 2004: Oct 11.

Monterroso, Augusto. *Mouvement perpétuel*. Translated by Christine Monot. Albi, France: Éditions du passage Nord / Ouest, 2004: Oct 13; Nov 21.

Monzón, Roberto. *Dame Más tiempo vida*. Colloquia, Guatemala: Ediciones de la Anormalidad, 2002: Feb 24; Mar 20, 22, 23; Apr 3.

Neruda, Pablo. *Canto General*. Translated by Jack Schmitt. Berkeley, CA: University of California Press, 1991: Jan 9, 11, 12, 17, 22, 24, 29; Feb 10; Apr 11; May 11, 17; Aug 5; Sept 12; Nov 25; Dec 14, 28, 29.

BIBLIOGRAPHY

Neruda, Pablo. *The Captain's Verses.* Translated by Donald D. Walsh. New York: New Directions, 1972.

Neruda, Pablo. *Passions and Impressions.* Edited by Matilde Neruda and Miguel Otero Silva. Translated by Margaret Sayers Peden. New York: Farrar, Strauss, and Giroux, 1983: Jan 2; Feb 9; Mar 4, 5; May 18; Jun 22; Nov 5, 19; Dec 1, 15, 25.

Neruda, Pablo. *Twenty Love Poems and a Song of Despair.* Translated by W.S. Merwin. New York: Penguin, 2004: Jan 5, 23; Feb 26; Mar 1; Aug 4, 11; Sept 6, 13; Dec 13.

Olivera Grotti, Gladys. *Aux Abords de l'identité latino-américaine.* Paris: L'Harmattan, 2003: Feb 14; May 30; Jun 23; Jul 24; Aug 14, 21; Sept 4; Nov 27; front endpaper.

Pacheco, José Emilio. *City of Memory and Other Poems.* Translated by Cynthia Steele and David Lauer. San Francisco, CA: City Lights, 1997: Jan 6.

Paz, Octavio, and Marie José Paz. *Figures and Figurations.* Translated by Eliot Weinberger. New York: New Directions, 2002: Jul 26.

Paz, Octavio. *Itinerary.* Translated by Jason Wilson. New York: Harcourt, 1999: Mar 2; Apr 25, 26; Jul 8, 19; Oct 4–6, 8, 15, 23, 25, 26, 29; Nov 20; Dec 6.

Paz, Octavio. *The Labyrinth of Solitude.* Translated by Lysander Kemp. New York: Grove Press, 1985: Feb 18; Mar 6, 21; Apr 8, 14; May 15; Jun 8, 12, 14, 20; Jul 10, 11, 13, 28; Aug 9; Sept 1, 3; Oct 16, 21; Nov 3.

Paz, Octavio. *Libertad bajo Palabra.* Madrid: Catedra, 1988: Jan 13; Mar 3, 16, 17; Apr 18; May 2, 6, 9, 12; Jul 22; Oct 28; Dec 4.

Paz, Octavio. *The Monkey Grammarian.* Translated by Helen Lane. New York: Arcade, 1990: Jan 14; Mar 28; Jun 4; Dec 24.

Paz, Octavio. *One Earth, Four or Five Worlds.* Translated by Helen Lane. Orlando, FL: Harcourt Brace Jovanovich, 1985: Oct 14, 24.

Paz, Octavio. *Pierre de soleil.* Translated by Benjamin Péret. Paris: Gallimard, 1990: May 16.

Paz, Octavio. *A Tree Within.* Translated by Eliot Weinberger. New York: New Directions, 1988: Jan 18; Feb 23; Mar 19; Apr 21, 23, 28; Jun 13, 18, 19; Jul 18, 30; Aug 7, 10; Oct 2; Nov 4; Dec 23.

Perdomo, Maria Teresa. *Periferias.* Mexico: Universidad Michoacana de San Nicolas de Hildago, 1982: Feb 12; Dec 12.

Poumier, Maria. *Poésie Salvadorienne du XXème siècle.* Geneva, Switzerland: Patino, 2002: Feb 3, 27; Aug 13.

Quino, Le Monde de Mafalda. *vol. 5 of Malfalda.* Translated by J. and A.M. Meunier. Grenoble, France: Glénat, 1999: April 7.

Resendiz Carmona, Roberto. *De peces y de colores.* Sociedad mexicana de geografía y Estadística, Lic. Alfonso García Robles-Corresponsalía en Zamora, Mexico, 1999: Mar 30; Aug 28.

Roa Bastos, Augusto. *Son of Man.* Translated by Rachel Caffyn. New York: Monthly Review Press, 1988: May 4.

Sabines, Jaime. *Uno es el poeta antología.* Edited by Carmen Alemany Bay. Madrid: Visor Libros, 2003: Aug 15; Dec 22.

Sepúlveda, Luis. *The Old Man who Read Love Stories.* Translated by Peter Bush. New York: Harcourt Brace, 1993: Jun 17; Nov 2.

Thomson, Magdalena. *El silencio es un cisne de sal.* Buenos Aires, Argentina: Edición Imaginarias, 1996: Jul 5.

Vargas Llosa, Mario. *Making Waves.* Translated by John King. London: Faber and Faber, 1996: Sept 5; Nov 16.

Vargas Llosa, Mario. *Who Killed Palomino Molero?.* Translated by Alfred Mac Adam. New York: Farrar, Straus, Giroux, 1987: Jul 27.

Verani, Hugo J. *Les Prix Nobels de littérature Hispano-Américain.* Geneva, Switzerland: Patiño, 1994: May 24; Jul 31.

INTERNET SOURCES

Atkinson, Patricio. www.ana.com.gt: Apr 17.

Buarque, Cristovam. ecolesdifferentes.free.fr/AMAZONIE.htm: Sept 18.

Câmara, Dom Hélder. www.domhelder.com.be: May 13; Jun 25; Sept 9, 19, 28; Oct 7.

Cerna, Ismael. www.geocities.com/jupagg/poeismaelcerna.html: Apr 12.

Guillén, Nicolas. www.members.tripod.com/poesialat/guillen.html: Jun 11.

Manzanero, Armando. ingeb.org/songs/contigo.html: Aug 6.

Martí, José. www.cubacenter.org/inside_cuba/marti.html: Nov 17.

Mayor, Federico. unesdoc.unesco.org/images/0011/001140/114002Fo.pdf: Sept 29; Oct 22.

Neruda, Pablo. www.neruda.uchile.cl/critica/silvacastro.html: Feb 13; Jul 14.

Neruda, Pablo. www.culturek.net/index_section_.php?record ID=218&MM_section=Arts: Dec 2.

Neruda, Pablo. "Crepusculario" (1919). www.literatura.us/neruda/melisanda.html: Jul 2; Dec 30.

Neruda, Pablo. www.loquesomos.org/elpalabro/poesia/poesia.htm: May 31.

Paz, Octavio. Compiled by Roly Canteros. "Del Poder, el Dinero, la Política y la Sociedad." Buenos Aires, Argentina: www.cantervill.com.ar/fyp/z-pod4.htm: Oct 27.

ACKNOWLEDGMENTS

To Dante Valdez Pedroni in Guatemala.
Diego & Christiane Gradis in Switzerland.
Alain & Virginie de Borchgrave d'Altena in Belgium,
*   who opened the doors to Latin America for us.*

THE FOLLOWING SHARERS OF WISDOM formed a vast network of friends and individuals who helped, supported, advised, and guided us in the making of this book. We wish to extend them our deepest thanks.

IN BELGIUM:

Mr. Armando Ortuño Yañez, Bolivian ambassador to the Kingdom of Belgium and the Grand Duchy of Luxembourg.
Mrs. Ana Isabel de la Goublaye, second secretary for Cultural Affairs.
Mr. Nicolas Echavarria Mesa, former Colombian ambassador in Brussels.
Mrs. Laura Pujols, second secretary for Consular Affairs at the Cuban embassy in Brussels.
Mr. Méntor Villagomez-Merino, ambassador of Ecuador to the Kingdom of Belgium and the Grand Duchy of Luxembourg.
Mr. Edmond Mulet, former Guatemalan ambassador to Brussels, Special Representative for the Secretary General and United Nations Mission for Stabilization in Haiti (MINUSTAH), and his wife Karen Lind Sverdrup de Mulet.
Mr. Jorge Molina Santizo, first secretary and consul for Guatemala.
Mrs. Teodolinda Banegas de Makris, former ambassador for Honduras.
Mrs. Maria de Lourdes Dieck Assad, Mexican ambassador to the Kingdom of Belgium and the Grand Duchy of Luxembourg, and her husband Mr. Pedro Quintanilla Gomez-Noriega.
Mr. Abel Escartin Molina, second secretary for Economic Affairs at the Mexican Embassy in Brussels.
Mr. Pablo Garrido Arauz, ambassador of Panama to the Kingdom of Belgium and the Grand Duchy of Luxembourg.
Mr. Luis Chuquihuara, Peruvian ambassador to the

Kingdom of Belgium and the Grand Duchy of
Luxembourg, and Mr. Gilberto Guevara, second
secretary (cultural attaché) at the Peruvian embassy
in Brussels.

IN BOLIVIA:
Gustavo Aguilar Salvador, Regional Coordinator for
MUSEF in Sucre.
Mr. Juan Angola Maconde, Afro-Bolivian
representative of the Yungas.
Mrs. Cristina Bubba, ethnologist in La Paz.
Mr. Dario Espinosa, specialist of the Quechua
language in La Paz.
Mr. Alain Fouquet, ambassador of France.
Mr. Hugo Fernandez, Mr. Felipe Santos Quispe, and
Mr. Rodolfo Quisbert Peña of the Andean and
Aymara Peoples Oral History Workshop (THOA)
in La Paz.
Mr. Juan Carlos Schulze of PRAIA, the regional
support program for the indigenous people of
Amazonia in La Paz.

IN CUBA:
Gloria de la Luz at the Cuban International Press
Center in Havana.

IN ECUADOR:
Mrs. Melva Patricia Gualinga Montalvo of the
Regional Council's Legal and Associated Department.
Mr. Silvio David Malaver Santi, a member of Atayak
(a group of former wise men charged with
perpetuating the tradition) and of the Sarayaku
community.

IN EL SALVADOR:
Mr. Ricardo Olmedo, Mrs. Julia Pons, and Mrs. Rita
Pons, connoisseurs of Salvadoran popular tradition.

IN FRANCE:
Mr. Fernando de Almeida, specialist in Latin
American studies in Paris.
Mr. Bruno Baudry of Fujifilm France.
Mr. Guy Bourreau, marketing director for Canon
France.
Mr. Jean-François Camp, director of the DUPON lab
in Paris.
Mr. Guy Frangeul and Mr. Jean Michel Krief,
photography department heads at Objectif Bastille
in Paris.

Mr. Corneille Jest, researcher with the CNRS in Paris.
Mrs. Maria Cecilia Laverde Montoya, Colombian
psychologist in Grenoble.
Mr. Guillermo Uribe, director of the Social Sciences
Research Group for Latin America (GRESAL), senior
lecturer in sociology in Grenoble.

IN GUATEMALA:
The Association for the Prevention of Delinquency
(APREDE) in Antigua.
Mr. Patricio Atkinson, founder of the God's Child
project in Antigua.
Mr. Pedro Camaja, director of the *Fundebase*
association in Sacatapequez.
Mrs. Ana Maria Pedroni, literature professor in
Antigua, and Sergio Pedroni.
Mr. David Pinto Reyfeo of the University of San
Carlos in Ciudad de Guatemala.
Marco Antonio Sagastume Gemmelle, coordinator at
the University of San Carlos in Guatemala City and
adviser to the Grand Confederation of Guatemala's
principal Aj'quijab.

IN MEXICO:
Julieta Gil Elorduy, ethnologist, and the staff of the library of the National Museum of Anthropology in Mexico City.
Mrs. Silvia Rojo Lugo and Mrs. Gloria Amtmann Aguilar, specialists in Mexican popular singers in Mexico City.
Maria del Perpetuo Socorro Villareal Escarrega, National Coordinator for the National Institute of Anthropology and History in Mexico City.
Mrs. Nicole Wyrsch, consultant to the Swiss Embassy in Mexico City.

IN PERU:
Mrs. Gloria Caceres Varga, Quechua professor in Ayacucho.
Mr. Dario Espinoza, historian and founder of the SAMI Quecha bilingual cultural center in Cuzco.
Mr. Juan de Dios Yapita, professor at the Aymara Language and Literature Institute in Lima.
Mr. José Ramón López de León, Mexican consul in Lima.
Mr. Grimaldo Rengifo and Mr. Jorge Ishizawa, founders of the Andean Project for Peasant Technologies (PRATEC) in Lima.
Mr. Hector Flores of the NASA Group for Andean Cultural Affirmation in Puno.
Mr. Carlos Vasquez Corrales, director of international cooperation in Lima.

IN SPAIN:
Mrs. Blanca Polio, a psychologist and psychoanalyst at the University of Barcelona, and Eduardo Polio.

IN SWITZERLAND:
Mrs. Madeleine Viviani, Secretary General of the Swiss Commission for UNESCO.

IN THE UNITED STATES:
Mrs. Veronica Milchorena, Director of the Miami Short Film Festival.
Mrs. Evelyn Pons, a researcher in the oral traditions of El Salvador.

AND, FOLLOWING THE COURSE OF OUR TRAVELS:
Mrs. Cecilia Antequera Camacho in Sucre.
Mrs. Carmiña Cabrera Essanguino and her cousin Mr. Walter Kuljis Fishner in Santa Cruz.
Jennifer Centy Paco and Luis Juares Pinto in Arequipa.
Mrs. Andrés Chacon in Sucre.
Mr. René Collet and Anna, who left us far too early, for the wonderful expeditions we undertook in Chilean Patagonia and the Cordillera Apolobamba in Bolivia, joined by Mr. Philippe Allibert and Mr. Philippe Modéré, who, sadly, are also no longer with us.
Mr. Jose Carlos Da Conceicao Ferreira in Salvador da Bahia.
Mrs. Claudia Lucia Diaz Lopez and her family in Antigua.
Mrs. Gil Dumas in Neuchâtel.
Mrs. Martha Garcia and Mr. Thierry Legros in Nice.
Mrs. Gitte Elisabeth Moeller.
Mr. Alberto Rafael Gonzales Figueroa, salsa dance teacher in Antigua.
Mr. Geovany Ranjel Grijalva in Panajachel.
Guia and Tomas Mayo Vargas in Potosi.
Mrs. Margarita Miguelanez Compuzano in Madrid.
Renaud and Claudia Neubauer in Quito.
Mrs. Suzanne Pons Fernandez in Cayenne.
Mr. Michel Pons in Paris.

Mr. Benigno Ramos Challco in Arequipa.
Mr. Ulio Santander in La Paz.
Mr. Gustavo Adolfo Terceros in Uyuni.
Mrs. Gabriela Perez Palma y Elorduy in Brussels.
Mrs. Helen Rios Filipps, Mr. Alexandru Ureche, and
Mr. Mircea Hainaru in Constanta, Rumania.
Mr. Eric Van Hecke in Rio de Janeiro.

And, finally, those who took it upon themselves to
bring exposed film back from Peru, Guatemala, and
Brazil: Mrs. Aziza Aarab, Mr. Sébastien Jacques, Mrs.
Helène Toury, and Mr. Eric Van Hecke.

The following individuals participated in the making
of *Revelations: Latin American Wisdom for Every Day:*

LITERARY RESEARCH:
Virginie de Borchgrave d'Altena, journalist
specializing in Latin culture.
Clara Guiomar, ethnologist of the Quecha language
and civilization.
Anne Le Noël, journalist specializing in
communication.

PHOTO ASSISTANTS:
Nora Delgado Vega, Clara Guiomar, and Gaëlle
Jacques.

PHOTO COORDINATION:
Guy de Régibus.

AT THE FÖLLMI STUDIO:
Viviane Bizien, Emmanuelle Courson, Marie-
Christine De Sa, Chantal Dubois, Laurence
Duchemin, Corinne Sédik, Nicolas Pasquier, François
Watel, and Stéphane Méron.

AT ÉDITIONS DE LA MARTINIÈRE:
Emmanuelle Halkin, Caroline Scotto, Valérie Roland,
Dominique Escartin, Marianne Lassandro, Agnès
Poirson, and Cécile Vandenbroucque.

This book is the fourth volume in the Offerings for Humanity series
that promotes humanity's spiritual heritage.

This project was made possible by the generous support of an
anonymous donor and by Lotus & Yves Mahé,

 and UNESCO's Swiss commission

The Offerings for Humanity project
is also generously supported by

 FUJIFILM

With the participation as well of
DUPON Laboratory

and Canon

and GRANDS
REPORTAGES
EXPLORER LE MONDE

To learn more about the "Offerings for Humanity" project: www.sagesses.com

The photographer's productions, projects, and advice: www.olivier-follmi.com

HOPE (Organization for People and Education): www.hope-organisation.com

Olivier Föllmi's agency in Paris, RAPHO: www.rapho.com

Translated from the Spanish by Asa Zatz and from the French by Nicholas Elliott

First published in the United Kingdom in 2006 by
Thames & Hudson Ltd, 181A High Holborn,
London WC1V 7QX

www.thamesandhudson.com

British Library Cataloguing-in-Publication Data
A catalogue record for this book is available from the British Library

ISBN-13: 978-0-500- 54322-1

ISBN-10: 0-500-54322-4

Printed and bound in France - n° L20617G

I have not come to resolve

anything.

I have come here to sing

and for you to sing with me.

—Pablo Neruda